Prayers That Open Heaven

❧

Apostle Jamie T. Pleasant; Ph.D.

Prayers That Open Heaven

Apostle Jamie T. Pleasant; Ph.D.

Prayers That Open Heaven

Copyright © 2009 by Apostle Jamie T. Pleasant; Ph.D.

All rights reserved. No portion of this book may be reproduced, stored in a retrieval system or transmitted in any form or by any means — electronic, mechanical, photocopy, recording or other — except for brief quotation in printed reviews, without the prior written authorization of the author.

Unless otherwise indicated, scripture quotations are taken from the Holy Bible, New International Version.

ISBN 1449541402

Get Ready to See Heaven Open

Do you want your prayers to be heard and answered by God? Do you want to be sure your prayer time isn't wasted going through a wishful, whimsical exercise with the hope that something might happen? Do you really want to learn what happens when you pray? Do you want to know the process that takes place during prayer?

If you often ask yourself these questions, then Prayers That Open Heaven will unlock the secrets of prayer in your life. Apostle Jamie T. Pleasant debuts with his first book that will teach you how to develop a more powerful and effective prayer life. This book is designed for personal and small group Bible study. Each week, you'll see your prayer time with God and your overall perspective on prayer transform. Chapter exercises and key points will help you make the most of your study time as you delve into the eight truths of prayer that open heaven.

Dedication

To my daddy Anthony T. Pleasant who was a perfect example to me of a real man. I will never forget the sacrifices and personal time you spent with me as a child. Daddy, I am still trying to live up to the perfect example of a father that you were to me. Rest in peace!

To my wife Kimberly (God gave me His best in you!), my two sons, Christian and Zion, and daughter, Nicara (you all are the wind beneath my wings). All I want to do is leave a legacy of Godliness to you.

To my mother Bertha Mae Pleasant, I thank God for the little time we spent together. Though it was only a few short years, your example of how to save money and operate businesses has prepared me for all the successes I enjoy to this day.

To my mother Alberta Gray, thank you for loving me and allowing me to have a chance at a great life. It was all God's divine plan and as a result, we are both blessed. I love you with all my heart!

To the Holy Spirit, Christ and Jehovah, what can I say except if it was not for you, I would be nothing. This book is the handiwork of your wisdom, grace and anointing!

To Ruby Grant, you gave me the two best things in this world I could ever have….your daughter to marry and your love…Priceless!

To the New Zion Christian Church Family, especially, Celeste Dickson, LaCretia Jones, Latoya Dockery, Deacon Lyndon Early, Minister Lawrence Gibbs III, Sequester McKinney, Deacon John F. Kennedy, Karon "superman" Riley, John and Rhonda Walker and Janet Peterson (what faith you have!).

To the Pleasant Family of Pinewood, South Carolina (Oh how I love you all so much!): Reggie and Jessica Pleasant, Sanders Pleasant (the Patriarch!), Richard Pleasant, The Brunson Family (where would I be without you!), Aunt Bernice Brunson, (my third mother), Aunt Thelma Sumter, Robert Sumter (my brother and I love you so!), Aunt Jesse Mae, "Mellie Mel" Melvin Davis (my big brother!) and Bertha Dinkins (my heart forever!).

To my Benedict College family, Norman Snipes, Julie Bennett, Loretta Herrin, Joyce Buxton, Rev. John Preacher (you saw great things in me before I saw them in myself); Clemson University, Coach Danny Ford (A leader of men), Coach Brother Bill Oliver, Coach Woody McCorvey, Terry Kinard (my hero and living legend), Coach Dabo Swinney, Jesse Hatcher (so much wisdom!), Ren Windham (my girl!), Dexter Davis, Keith Jennings, Gene Beasley, Richard Smith, Kellye Whitaker, Danny Buggs, Richard Reese (you started my corporate career at Clemson), Randy Anderson (Audi 4000), Al Mathiasen, Ken Harmon (you believed in me and gave me a chance); Clark Atlanta University (You gave me my confidence and vision), Ed Davis, Raphael Boyd, Alice Cayson, The late great Alex Williams (you taught me how to make it happen sir!); Georgia Tech, Naresh Malholtra and Fred Allvine.

To Erika, Wendy, Lois, Wanda, Chris, Joe Louis, Ola Mae, Susan, Gloria and Toney Jr. (my brothers and sisters…I love you all); Rev. Cornelius Henderson, Rev. Leroy Rankin (my rock), Ruben Perry (a spiritual father to me), Angelia (you shaped me into a man of excellence!), Cleve Pounds and Coach Shann Hart.

To everyone that made a positive impact in my life. If I have forgotten anyone please charge it to my old age and not my heart.

Humbly Yours, Jamie

Getting the Most from
Prayers That Open Heaven

Congratulations on purchasing this book! Get ready take your prayer life to the next level. You can use this book for personal or group study. All of the scriptures are from the New International Version, or NIV Bible translation. You'll find it helpful to have your Bible handy as you study.

This book includes nine chapters — perfect for a week-by-week study. Eight of the chapters include key truths that show you how to get heaven to open when you pray. The last chapter recaps what you've learned. In addition, you'll find:

- Key points. Each time you see lines above and below a point, this point is important for you to note and is reinforced at the end of the chapter. For example,

  When we pray, heaven literally opens up.

- Exercises. The blank spaces allow you to write your thoughts and reflect on key points within the chapter. Completing the exercises within the chapter and at the end of each chapter will help you reinforce what you learn.

1

When We Pray, Heaven Opens Up

When all the people were being baptized, Jesus was baptized too. And as he was praying, heaven was opened.

Luke 3:21

When we pray, heaven literally opens up.

One of the greatest secrets of prayer in the Bible is revealed in **Luke 3:21**:

When all the people were being baptized, Jesus was baptized too. And as he was praying, heaven was opened.

As Christ Jesus was praying, heaven was opened. What a revelation for us to know that every single time we pray, heaven is opened up, right in front of our eyes!

Visioning is the key to unlocking the supernatural world of prayer and the things of God.

The first thing we must do in order to begin to have a more productive prayer life is to envision that when we pray, heaven is opened up for us. Take a moment and look up wherever you are and picture heaven opening up. Believe it or not, that is exactly what happens when you pray. However, the main point in this exercise is for you to know that what you envision becomes a reality in your prayer life. The first training you must undergo in order to become a powerful praying person, is to begin to see through visioning exercises, that heaven does actually open up. Visioning is the key to unlocking the supernatural world of prayer and the things of God.

Try this exercise for starters. Look at the cube below. Don't just look for a few seconds. Look at it without any interruptions for at least 45 seconds without moving your eyes off of it. Go ahead and start now.

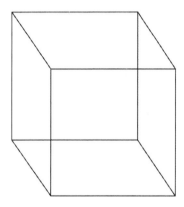

Did you notice anything peculiar happen? You should have. Write down what you saw as you focused on the cube.

_____
_____
_____
_____
_____

The openings of the cube should have changed.

The cube may have even shifted positions on the paper right in front of your eyes. It might have even turned around completely as you stared at it. First, you may have seen an opening up top. Then, if you kept looking, it may have shifted to the left or right or bottom. Did that happen to you? If not, go back and practice this visioning exercise. Until you can look at this still image on paper, and see it move, you are not ready to see heaven open up when you look to the sky while you are praying.

If we can't see spiritual things with our natural eyes, they will never become a reality in our natural life.

Yes, heaven opens up and has always opened up. But, we must know that it happens and see that it happens, in order for effective, powerful prayer to occur in our lives. An interesting thought here is to know that in order for super and great things to happen in our world, we must naturally see supernatural things before they can occur. *Did you get that?* In other words, we must see naturally, what the naked eye can't see in order for our naked eye to finally see supernatural things. Another way to look at it is this way: We must begin to see that which is always there, that which has always been there and that which will always be there, that our normal eyes can't see. If we can't see these spiritual things with our natural eyes, they will never become a reality in our natural life.

Problems, troubles and challenges we see and face daily are temporary, not permanent.

Now take a look at **2 Corinthians 4:18**. It says:

So we fix our eyes not on what is seen, but on what is unseen. For what is seen is temporary, but what is unseen is eternal.

What a powerful scripture for us! Notice God's truth here. The scripture says that we did not create something that was not there. The scripture says it has always been there, waiting for us to focus on it long enough so that it will become a reality. Now, to go a little deeper, look at the truth that the things we should focus on are the permanent eternal things of God that are not seen easily with natural eyes.

His voice, presence, blessings, love, peace and power that we can't seem to put our hands on are eternal.

What a blessing to know that there is a permanent reality waiting for us beyond the temporary things we may be experiencing in our daily lives now. Next, to make this point clearer to you, think about some of the many things you may be focusing on in your life. You may be focusing on bills, car problems, an exam, loneliness, health problems, etc. The key truth here is that all the problems, troubles and challenges we see and face daily are temporary, not permanent. His voice, presence, blessings, love, peace and power that we can't seem to put our hands on are eternal. We must focus and desperately look for unseen permanent things from God.

In the blank spaces on the next page, write down the number of hours a day you usually experience or focus on things that make you uncomfortable, nervous and stressed out. Next, write down the number of hours a day you focus on the goodness of God, the blessings of God, the deliverance of God, the miracles of God and the steadfastness of God.

I usually spend _____ hours a day experiencing trouble in my life.

I usually spend _____ hours a day focusing on a solution to the trouble in my life.

I usually spend _____ hours a day experiencing the goodness, blessing and power of God in my life.

I usually spend _____ hours a day praying to God that His blessings will be revealed in my life.

We need to focus more on the things of God rather than the uncomfortable, troubling events we may be experiencing in our daily lives.

How did you do with the exercise? Did you find out that you spend more time experiencing and focusing on problems and how to solve them than you do on the goodness of God and His blessings? If so, that may be why you are going through so many problems and heartaches. You simply focus on them too much. We need to know that what we focus on becomes our reality. We need to focus on the things of God even in the midst of experiencing uncomfortable events. **Philippians 4:8** says,

Finally, brothers, whatever is true, whatever is noble, whatever is right, whatever is pure, whatever is lovely, whatever is admirable — if anything is excellent or praiseworthy — think about such things.

Our reality becomes what we focus on, and what we focus on becomes our reality.

We must now begin to tap into the power of prayer and hit the unseen realm of blessings. And as we pray, we see heaven open up for us and release beautiful things to us like peace, joy, patience and power. What a blessing it will be when in the middle of trying times, we can pull away and reach a place of eternal bliss in the midst of heartache, pain and trouble. That place is real, and it is called prayer. Specifically, it is called a prayer closet.

A major breakthrough in understanding prayer is that there should be less talking by us and more listening to Him.

Looking back at Luke 3:21, we see Christ Jesus praying and heaven is opened. He is about to begin His earthly mission. He needs to know for sure that His Father is with Him. He needs to know that He has been given power to be successful through the Holy Spirit. He needs to know that as He experiences resistance and trouble from His enemies, He will be delivered. He needs to know what His outcome will be before He starts out. Thus, as He is being baptized and prays, He watches eagerly to be very sure His time and protection has truly come. He can't guess about it. He can't hope and be wrong about it or even dream about it. Christ Jesus must know He is walking in divine purpose and protection and that it is time for Him to begin His mission on earth.

As He enters prayer, He focuses so intently on heaven that He finally sees it open, and then He hears the voice of His Father say,

…and the Holy Spirit descended on him in bodily form like a dove. And a voice came from heaven: "You are my Son, whom I love; with you I am well pleased." Luke 3:22

Notice here that we don't see or hear Jesus speaking. He is just looking toward heaven, and all of a sudden, it opens up for Him and the Father speaks. A major breakthrough in understanding prayer is that there should be less talking by us and more listening to Him.

We must get to the stage where we can just stand up, focus and aim at heaven, watch it open up and wait for the voice of the Father to speak.

What a powerful prayer life Christ Jesus must have had, to be able to just stand up, vision and focus at heaven and the voice of the Father speaks. We must get to that stage and place where we can just stand up, focus and aim at heaven, watch it open up and wait for the voice of our heavenly Father to speak to us as well. It can happen. All we have to do is focus, fix and wait.

Chapter 1 Review and Exercise

Now, let's review the key points of this chapter.
1. When we pray, heaven literally opens up.
2. Visioning is the key to unlocking the supernatural world of prayer and the things of God.
3. If we can't see spiritual things with our natural eyes, they will never become a reality in our natural life.
4. Problems, troubles and challenges we see and face daily are temporary, not permanent.
5. His voice, presence, blessings, love, peace and power that we can't seem to put our hands on are eternal.
6. We need to focus more on the things of God rather than the uncomfortable troubling events we may be experiencing in our daily lives.
7. Our reality becomes what we focus on, and what we focus on becomes our reality.
8. A major breakthrough in understanding prayer is that there should be less talking by us and more listening to Him.
9. We must get to the stage where we can just stand up, focus and aim at heaven, watch it open up and wait for the voice of the Father to speak.

Spiritual Exercise

1. Write a prayer to God, and ask Him to give you the ability to fix, focus and wait on Him to speak as heaven is opened up to you.

   _____
   _____
   _____
   _____
   _____

2. Next, quiet yourself and look up to heaven and envision it opening. Wait and be patient and write down what God says to you.

   _____
   _____
   _____
   _____
   _____

2

Prayer Changes Things, And You Should Change Too

As he was praying, the appearance of his face changed, and his clothes became as bright as a flash of lightning.

Luke 9:29

Prayer Changes Things, and You Should Change Too

As we pray, change immediately begins to have a positive impact on our situations and circumstances.

If you were to ask your family members, friends, coworkers and even fellow church members if they believe that prayer changes things, the majority of them would most likely agree with you quickly. However, if you were to ask if they believe that prayer can change things during the actual prayer experience, you might get a different response. While most people are very confident that prayer can change their situations and circumstances, they are very hesitant and cautious about expecting to see a change while they are in the process of praying.

However, there is great news concerning our prayer time that we spend with God. The good news is that as we pray, change immediately begins to have a positive impact on our situations and circumstances.

Prayer has a profound positive impact on our spirits, minds, souls and bodies.

Also, it is important for us to know that when we are in the middle of praying, prayer has a profound positive impact on our spirits, minds, souls and bodies.

Take a look at **Luke 9:28-29**. It says,

About eight days after Jesus said this, he took Peter, John and James with him and went up onto a mountain to pray. As he was praying, the appearance of his face changed, and his clothes became as bright as a flash of lightning.

We can see here that Jesus is about to let Peter, John and James in on one of the greatest secrets about prayer. Many times in the Bible we see Christ going off alone to pray. However, there is something different about His prayer time in this scripture. He wants them to watch and learn how He enters prayer and understand the benefits of such a deep involvement in the prayer activity.

In Luke 9:29, the key words we should focus on are, **"as he was praying"**. It was **"as he was praying,"** that the appearance of His face changed. This is a beautiful example for us to change the way we approach and conduct personal prayer. We should expect, at the very least, our face or disposition to change as we are praying. It is not Christ's intent to teach us and show us what might happen after we pray. It is His purpose to show us what will happen as we are praying. It is His intent to show us what takes place every time we pray.

God's presence, our spirit, our natural body, our mental state, our emotional state, our outlook on life, our mood, our character and our attitude make up the Nine Prayer Points of Completeness that must unfold in order for positive change to take place in our lives.

We should watch closely and know with confidence that one of the first things we should expect to change during our personal prayer time is our disposition. Disposition is defined as the predominant or prevailing tendency of one's spirit, natural, mental and emotional outlook or mood, characteristic or attitude. The power in the definition of disposition is that there is a progressive unfolding of the Nine Prayer Points of Completeness that take place within ourselves as we pray. The Nine Prayer Points of Completeness that unfold within us as we pray have a direct effect on how we respond to things in our daily lives.

The Nine Prayer Points of Completeness that we go through during actual prayer time are explained as follows.

- First, it is God's influence on our spirit that impacts our natural body.

Prayer Changes Things, and You Should Change Too

- Next, it is our spirit that produces the mental state that we operate in, which determines our emotional response to things, which dictates our outlook on life.

- Our outlook on life will positively or negatively impact our overall mood, which will ultimately define our character, which will in turn create our attitude toward life and people.

- Finally, our attitude toward life and people determines how we handle things we are faced with in this world and how we respond to people.

Nine Prayer Points of Completeness

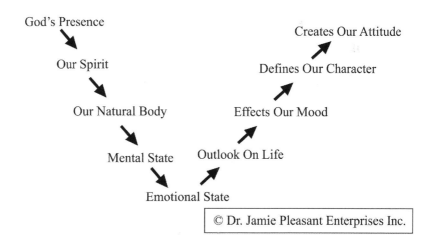

© Dr. Jamie Pleasant Enterprises Inc.

Prayer Changes Things, and You Should Change Too

Our outward attitude is only a reflection of our inner spirit being influenced by the presence of God.

Look at the Nine Prayer Points of Completeness more closely. Notice how we can expect an immediate change in our spirit first. That is, we should know and feel that we have come into the presence of the Almighty God. Second, our entire natural being should begin to calm down and settle into the awareness of the Almighty God, Christ and the Holy Spirit. Next, our mind should naturally relax and center to make the spiritual reality of God accessible to us. As our mind engages into processing the spiritual things of God, so that they can become a natural reality to us, our emotions are influenced by the state of our mind and reordered to a place of peace, trust and tranquility.

Then, as our emotions are being shaped by the awareness of God's presence in the deepest parts of our soul, our outlook will suddenly change to a positive position. This is when what is divine and hidden on the inside of us will now be reflected in our actions — fully expressed in our facial demeanor and total disposition. Next, as our outlook changes where it is publicly shared with those who come into contact with us, they will notice and compliment us on our pleasing character and attitude. But let's not forget that our outward attitude is only a reflection of our inner spirit being influenced by the presence of God.

The turning point to see change in our lives occurs at the emotional state of the Nine Prayer Points of Completeness during the prayer process.

The Nine Prayer Points of Completeness form the victory formation during the transfiguration process of prayer. This process produces a positive, prosperous outlook for us. Notice how the turning point in everything is hinged on our emotional state.

Also, we can't overlook the truth that nine is the number that represents the bearing of fruit in our lives. You should get ready now as you progress in this book to bear positive uplifting fruit in your life. Get ready to bear the fruit of joy. Get ready to bear the fruit of peace. Get ready to bear the fruit of prosperity. Get ready to bear the fruit of confidence. Get ready to bear the fruit of the Spirit which are stated in the scripture:

But the fruit of the Spirit is love, joy, peace, patience, kindness, goodness, faithfulness, gentleness and self-control. Against such things there is no law. Galatians 5:22-23

Look at how we should experience change while we are in the act of praying. These things should occur to us as we are in the act of praying. It is important to know that when we come out of

Prayer Changes Things, and You Should Change Too

prayer, the fruit of the Spirit should be reflected in our daily lives.

During prayer, once the fruit of the Spirit is produced in our lives, the natural laws of hurt, pain, disappointment, etc. can no longer operate to negatively affect us anymore.

Please pay special attention to what will happen at the end of our prayer experience when the fruit of the Spirit is manifested in our lives. The secret is found at the end of Galatians 5:23 where it says that against such things there is no law. How refreshing it is to know that when we give birth to the fruit of the Spirit during prayer, no natural law of hurt, pain, disappointment, despair or heartache can have a negative effect in our lives. The natural laws of hurt, pain, despair and heartache can't operate in our lives anymore to negatively affect us because the fruit of the Spirit governs our being and protects all external circumstances and situations that are trying to get into our minds, hearts and spirits.

Prayer should uproot every bitter root that we are experiencing in our lives.

Prayer Changes Things, and You Should Change Too

Our prayers should be fruitful in producing positive change in our lives regardless of what we are experiencing or going through at the present moment. In addition, prayer should uproot every bitter root that we are experiencing in our lives. Prayer should uproot all doubt, hurt, pain, disappointment and fear that we may have about something. Prayer should release the virtue of our heavenly Father through the Holy Spirit that is reflected in our disposition when we pray and also after we pray.

Prayer is the vehicle where what God has for us and wants to do through us, comes to us.

Focus must now be given to **Luke 9:29** where it says,

As he was praying, the appearance of his face changed, and his clothes became as bright as a flash of lightning.

Notice how not only did His face or disposition change, but His clothes changed as well. The truth revealed here is that during prayer not only are you experiencing a change, everything that is attached to you is now changing for the better also. Think about all the childhood doubts, letdowns, disappointments and hurts that just won't seem to let you go. Think about all the past things that seem to hang on to you. How refreshing it is to know that as you are praying and you begin to change, all evil and destructive things that you bring with you in prayer will change right before your eyes. These things will fall off of you in the middle of the transfiguration process of prayer.

What a blessing to know that we can take our problems, doubts and burdens to the Lord in prayer, leave them there and watch them be changed right in front of our eyes while we are still praying. Prayer is the vehicle where what God has for us and wants to do through us, comes to us.

God speaks to you, through you.

We should experience the miracle of change during prayer every time we pray. Change should not be something that we hope for after we pray. Prayer should produce change within us before we say Amen at the end of praying.

Try this exercise right now by beginning to pray. As you pray, hold your arms out with your palms up, keep your eyes open and picture heaven opening up to you. Next, just sit there and wait to hear God say something to you. He may speak out audibly to you, or He may speak quietly to you in your spirit. Don't make the mistake of hearing a voice in your head and think that it is just you talking to yourself. Most of the time, it is God speaking to you, through you. Yes! He speaks to you, through you. Center yourself and anticipate His voice. Once you hear from Him, write down below what He said to you. I promise that you are going to hear from God for yourself.

_____
_____
_____
_____
_____

Next, write what you felt in your body as you prayed with God.

_____
_____
_____
_____
_____

You might have felt goose bumps at the base of your neck or tingling sensations over your entire body. You might even have felt chills run up and down your spine. Your hands may become warm and feel like warm mittens have been placed on them.

What a blessing it is to know that you have been in the presence of the Almighty God Himself. Remember, when God

Prayer Changes Things, and You Should Change Too

shows up in your prayer time, you will feel Him, and you will experience change at that very moment.

Now that you have heard from God, felt Him and written what He has said to you, write below a response to Him. It is important to begin to write a response to everything that God says to you. It is God's way of knowing you are taking His precious time that He spends with you very seriously.

_____

_____

_____

_____

_____

Chapter 2 Review and Exercise

1. As we pray, change begins immediately to have a positive impact on our situations and circumstances.
2. Prayer has a profound positive impact on our spirits, minds, souls and bodies.
3. God's presence, our spirit, our natural body, our mental state, our emotional state, our outlook on life, our mood, our character and our attitude make up the Nine Prayer Points of Completeness that must unfold in order for positive change to take place in our lives.
4. Our outward attitude is only a reflection of our inner spirit being influenced by the presence of God.
5. The turning point to see change in our lives occurs at the emotional state of the Nine Prayer Points of Completeness during the prayer process.
6. During prayer, once the fruit of the Spirit is produced in our lives, the natural laws of hurt, pain, disappointment, etc. can no longer operate to negatively affect us anymore.
7. Prayer should uproot every bitter root that we are experiencing in our lives.
8. Prayer is the vehicle where what God has for us and wants to do through us, comes to us.

9. God speaks to you, through you.

Spiritual Exercise

1. Write down the key things you want God to reveal to you about being able to sense when change is taking place during your personal prayer time.

   _____
   _____
   _____
   _____
   _____

2. Write down the key things you learned in this chapter.

   _____
   _____
   _____
   _____
   _____

3

Our Prayers Are Answered Before We Pray

Before they call I will answer;
while they are still speaking I will hear.

Isaiah 65:24

Before we pray, God has already answered all of our questions or responded to all of our requests that we may bring forward in prayer.

Have you ever wondered how long it will take to get an answer from God when you pray? Do you want to know what must happen in order to get an answer from God? Do you want to know the proper things to do in order to hear from Him? Well, these questions will be answered in this chapter. In fact, in all honesty, all three of these questions can easily be answered according to **Isaiah 65:24**:

Before they call I will answer; while they are still speaking I will hear.

The beauty in this scripture is that it is not after prayer that we should anticipate an answer from God. It is not even during prayer we should expect an answer from God. The truth that is revealed in Isaiah 65:24 shows us that before we pray, God has already answered all of our questions or requests that we may bring forward in prayer. Literally, prayer is where the answer God has prepared for us before we were born is unveiled to meet us at a specific time in our lives. Wow! What a beautiful revelation.

All of the questions, doubts, concerns and decisions that we are pondering are all floating around as answers in spirit form waiting for God to reveal them at a specific time.

What an awesome truth to know that God has prepared answers for us before we are born to help us at a specific time in our present lives and circumstances. This means that all of the questions, doubts, concerns and decisions that we are pondering are all floating around as answers in spirit form. They are waiting to be revealed by God at the specific time He designed for us before we were born.

It is prayer that allows the transformation to take place from spiritual words that are difficult to interpret and hard to understand to natural words that can be interpreted and understood.

The key that transforms those answers, which are in spirit form, to a form we can understand is only possible through the process of prayer. It is prayer that allows this transformation to take place where what is spiritual can be interpreted and understood.

Our Prayers Are Answered Before We Pray

The reason we feel a need to pray is because God has released an answer that He wants to birth in us for our present situation.

A deeper look into Isaiah 65:24 shows us that the reason we feel a need to pray is because God has released an answer that He wants to birth in us for our present situation. It may simply be something that God wants to be revealed about our future, which has been purposed by Him.

When God has prepared an answer He wants us to hear and understand, He moves on us to begin the prayer process.

What an interesting thought to know: When God has prepared an answer He wants us to hear and understand, He moves on us to begin the prayer process. So, we should note that prayer is not something we actually initiate. God does the initiation of the prayer process between us and Him by moving on us with a desire to pray. Once we are moved to pray or drawn to pray, He then moves on us to ask the right questions in prayer so that the answer can be revealed to us clearly.

Prayer is similar to the game show Jeopardy. If you have ever watched Jeopardy, you know that the contestants must choose categories based on different topics and different levels of rewards. The key to playing the game is that the contestants must respond to the answers in each category in the form of a question. Although all of the categories are random, the levels of difficulty for each answer within a category become more difficult as the reward amounts get larger.

For example, the category may be "American History." A contestant may choose "American History" for $200. The $200 label is removed to reveal the answer, "He is the first African American to have a national holiday that is celebrated in the month of January." Notice that the answer is revealed when the contestant chooses that particular category. Next, the contestant must respond to the answer in the form of a question. The contestant then responds by asking, **"Who is Martin Luther King Jr.?"** Alex Trebek then will say, "That is the correct question." The contestant is awarded $200 for knowing the correct question to the answer.

Notice that the answer was already there before the contestants showed up that day on the show. The answers were there waiting to be revealed. However, no one would know the correct question to ask until the appropriate answer was chosen and revealed. The contestants must be at the show on their scheduled day in order to unveil the answers that were prepared for them before they got there that day. The correct question lets you know that you have found the correct answer.

God does this the same way for us. We are all contestants in a much more serious game called life. God has prepared answers for us that are waiting to be revealed to us at a specified time. Those answers, though already there and prepared for us, can't be revealed until we call on them. We can't call on them unless we are invited to participate in the game.

Contestants are invited by game show screeners to be tested in order to see if the contestants qualify to be on a particular show at a certain day and time. Contestants are prescreened to make sure they have a certain level of knowledge so that as they become qualified, their chances of being successful on the show are very good. Jeopardy screeners choose their invited contestants carefully so that the screeners are not embarrassed by contestants who are not able to ask the right questions to the predetermined answers. Contestants can either accept the invitation to come on the show, or they can refuse to respond to the invitation. However, the initial invitation comes from the people who own the show.

To take time out to pray is to take time out to participate in God's show of experiencing an eternal and satisfying life right now!

God owns this show that we participate in called life. He invites us to participate on His show where He will prepare us to be successful once we show up. Leaving where we are to get to the game show is the same thing as stopping what we are doing in our busy lives and taking time out to pray. To take time out to pray is to take time out to participate in God's show of experiencing an eternal and satisfying life right now!

Being obedient to His invitation to pray is the same as entering the game show, Jeopardy. We must make the effort to pack our bags, make flight plans and get to the show. In life, we must make time to make the trip in prayer in order to participate in what has already been prepared for us.

Notice, once a contestant arrives at the right place, when the correct question is asked; he or she is awarded the $200. The point here is that we must be at the correct place at the correct time in order to receive the reward for knowing the right question to ask.

Prayer is the place we must make an effort to get to if we want to be able to ask the right questions to the correct prepared answers that our loving Master has already ordained to be revealed.

Now get this! Many people watch and play Jeopardy on their television sets each day and ask the right questions to the revealed answers, but they don't get the reward of $200. The $200 is not theirs because it was not their game. The game and rewards belong to the person who accepts the invitation to play the game and puts forth the effort to get to the show.

Like the game of Jeopardy, prayer is the place we must make an effort to go to ask the right questions. Our loving Master has already ordained the correct prepared answers and is waiting to reveal them to us. Prayer is the place where we can now choose the right category and receive a reward if we know the right questions to ask. How beautiful it is to know that God has qualified us to come to a place in prayer knowing that we will be rewarded for asking the right questions. Wow! What a blessing that is to know.

God's answers are always in spiritual form, and they are constantly tugging away at us. Remember, He initiates prayer. He invites us to pray. These spiritual answers keep tugging at us and they won't go away until we enter into prayer. Once we are in prayer, we begin to ask the correct questions, the answers are revealed in front of our eyes and we are rewarded for asking the correct question. Our reward might be peace, a solution to a problem, a clear decision that had to be made, healing of cancer, the elimination of a hurt or pain or other things. However, we will feel better as we start hearing the answers. We then can move in the right direction and are better off during and after prayer than before the prayer process began.

Write a request to God below, and ask Him to begin to give you the ability to respond to His invitation of prayer time where answers can be revealed through you by asking the correct questions.

_____

_____

_____

_____

_____

Do you know the fact that you are making the request to ask God to give you the ability to respond to His invitation of prayer time is really God having prepared an answer for you already and has moved on your heart to request His prepared, preordained answer? That is very interesting, but it is true. That is exactly what has taken place. The very fact that you are reading this book says that God has prepared you for such a time as this to allow His answers to be revealed to you.

It is our speaking that causes God to hear.

The last part of Isaiah 65:24 states, **"while they are still speaking I will hear."** Pay attention to the fact that as we are still speaking in prayer, God hears. What a profound truth to know that it is our asking the correct questions that allows God to hear us. The truth revealed here is that it is not just our speaking to God that allows Him to hear us. No! It is our ability to ask Him the correct questions that allows Him to hear us and respond with what He has already prepared for us. In other words, if we don't ask the correct questions in our prayers, God doesn't hear us.

In prayer it is when we show God we are attentive to Him, He becomes attentive towards us.

The Hebrew word for hear is *shaw-mah'*. *Shaw-mah'* means, to give attention to. God is saying that only when we ask the right questions in prayer will He turn all His attention on us and focus intently on us.

In fact, it is only the correct questions that we ask that trigger His attention and intention toward us. It is only in prayer when we show God we are attentive to Him, He becomes attentive toward us. We show Him we are attentive by asking the right questions. He responds to us with the intent that the answers He reveals will move us in the direction of His blessings, plans and purposes that He preordained long before we were born.

Notice in **Romans 10:17**, the scripture says,

Consequently, faith comes from hearing the message, and the message is heard through the word of Christ.

The key point here is to understand that the word of Christ must be spoken first then the message is heard.

Spoken word of Christ → Message is Heard → Faith is Produced

Another way to look at this is to understand "*faith- producing prayer*" in its purest form. That is:

How To Get God To Answer Us In Prayer

If we speak the correct questions given to us by Christ
↓
God hears and gives his full attention to our message
↓
Then answers are revealed to us that will produce positive results in our situations

---

As we recite what Christ has put in us to ask the Father, the Father gives attention with the intent on producing a positive outcome or faith in our lives. Once again, all of this takes place while we are speaking or asking the correct questions to God our Father. A final point must be made here. That is, the Holy Spirit is the one who draws you to remember the correct questions to ask what Christ Jesus has placed on your heart, so that the Father will hear your prayers and act on your behalf. What a blessing to see the Father, Son and Holy Spirit in action to ensure our prayers are on point, on time and in truth.

Chapter 3 Review and Exercise

1. Before we pray, God has already answered all of our questions or responded to all of our requests that we may bring forward in prayer.
2. All of the questions, doubts, concerns and decisions that we are pondering are all floating around as answers in spirit form waiting for God to reveal them at a specific time.
3. It is prayer that allows the transformation to take place from spiritual words that are difficult to interpret and hard to understand to natural words that can be interpreted and understood.
4. The reason we feel a need to pray is because God has released an answer that He wants to birth in us for our present situation.
5. When God has prepared an answer He wants us to hear and understand, He moves on us to begin the prayer process.
6. To take time out to pray is to take time out to participate in God's show of experiencing an eternal and satisfying life right now!
7. Prayer is the place we must make an effort to get to if we want to be able to ask the right questions to the correct

prepared answers that our loving Master has already ordained to be revealed.

8. It is our speaking that causes God to hear.
9. In prayer it is when we show God we are attentive to Him, He becomes attentive towards us.

Spiritual Exercise

1. Write down the key things you want God to reveal to you about being able to sense when change is taking place during your personal prayer time.

   _____
   _____
   _____
   _____
   _____

2. Write down the key things you learned in this chapter.

   _____
   _____
   _____
   _____
   _____

4

When We Are "Still In Prayer," He Is Quick In Action

While I was still in prayer, Gabriel, the man I had seen in the earlier vision, came to me in swift flight about the time of the evening sacrifice. He instructed me and said to me, "Daniel, I have now come to give you insight and understanding."

Daniel 9:21-22

When We Are "Still In Prayer," He Is Quick In Action

We hear people always say that we must be still and wait on the Lord. Somehow, we take that to mean that God is always slow to answer our prayers or react to things we are dealing with or are seeking guidance on. However, a great truth exists in the fact that it is our ability to be still that allows Him to act swiftly. It is our stillness in prayer that causes Him to move into our lives very quickly. That's right! We need to learn how to practice stillness in our praying exercises.

It was Daniel's stillness in prayer that caused God's quick action.

Notice **Daniel 9:21-22**:

While I was <u>still in prayer</u>, Gabriel, the man I had seen in the earlier vision, came to me in <u>swift flight</u> about the time of the evening sacrifice. He instructed me and said to me, "Daniel, I have now come to give you insight and understanding."

Please pay special attention to verse 21 where it says that, "While I was still in prayer." This doesn't mean Daniel was praying, said what he wanted to say, and then afterwards, paused and waited to hear what God had to say. He wasn't looking up to heaven hoping to get some kind of instruction or divine word for his next move. Daniel was showing us how he was entering into a state of prayer where God was free to act on Daniel's requests immediately.

In fact, it was Daniel's stillness that caused God's quick action.

If we don't stop our busyness in prayer, God can't start His business of answering us in prayer.

To understand this better, we need to look at what the word, "still" means. The word still comes from the root word *daw-mam'*, which means to stop; quiet self, and hold peace. So, when we look closer at this word, we can see clearly now that as we approach prayer, we should stop, quiet ourselves and hold peace. Approaching prayer with this mindset will lead us to a place in prayer that will cause us to be still. In order to be still, we must stop worrying, stop doubting, stop lying, etc. We must also stop all of the busyness that distracts us from our prayer time with God. In fact, if we don't stop our <u>busyness</u> in prayer, God can't start His <u>business</u> of answering us in prayer. Watch this closely. We must have an attitude of quietness and peacefulness before we are able to enter the deepest realm of prayer, which is to be still.

Let's be honest with ourselves. Most of us come to prayer only when we are facing a crisis that places us in a state of uneasiness or stress. Most of the time, we react to the crisis by praying immediately. Please don't take this statement the wrong way. Whenever we are facing a crisis, we should enter into prayer to see what the Lord has to say. It is at the time when we are experiencing a crisis that we can talk to God and let Him know what is on our minds immediately.

What's important for us to know is that we shouldn't rush into prayer with the wrong attitude and disposition. It is okay to pray when we get angry. But we should wait until we have settled down and calmed our emotions, so we can pray the right things to God. We shouldn't enter into prayer in the heat of an argument with someone. We may become prone to ask God to do something mean or harmful to that person. Not only is this not Godly behavior, God won't move on such requests when we come to Him in that kind of state of mind.

That is why practicing the truth of "stillness" is key for us to get God's attention to help us with whatever our crisis may be. Being still in prayer also allows Him to answer us and give us the proper instruction on how to handle any situation we are facing.

To hold peace means to receive it, feel it, and then retain it.

Looking deeper at this powerful word "still," we find it means to hold peace. In order to allow God to move on our behalf, we must understand and know how to hold peace. The key here is to not just get to a place of peace while we pray or before we pray, but to get peace and hold on to it. To hold peace means to receive it, feel it, and then retain it. We must come in contact with peace and retain it in the midst of distractions during prayer. Our prayer only can be effective, and we can only hear from God, after we attain and can retain peace.

We must first receive and get the peace of God that can only come from God.

Peace can't be a fleeting, temporary thing. It must penetrate into the core of our very being. We must first receive and get the peace of God that can only come from God. Only then will we be able to get peace with God. Once we are at peace with God, then we will be at peace within ourselves. It is only after we are at peace with ourselves can we approach Him in prayer and have peace in our situations until they change.

Steps To Getting Peace From God and Holding On To It Until Change Comes

We must get…

- Peace from God
- Peace with God
- Peace within ourselves
- Peace in our situation even if change hasn't come yet

When We Are "Still In Prayer," He Is Quick In Action

When we share our deepest feelings with God, our honesty shows Him we trust Him. Then, we can get peace with God.

Too many of us fight within ourselves because we are not at peace with God. We are not at peace with God because we don't share our true feelings and concerns with Him. We seem to think that if we tell Him the truth, He will turn His ear away from us. So, we never feel comfortable sharing the deepest truths about ourselves with God. Some of us even think that our honesty might cause God to disqualify us as being worthy to Him. We also think that as we expose our true selves to Him, He will punish us and make us feel bad. These thoughts couldn't be farther from the truth.

The truth is, when we share our deepest feelings with God, our honesty shows Him we trust Him. Then, we can obtain peace with God. Telling God the truth shows Him we believe He is a God that forgives and we could never be perfect according to our standards. Being honest literally shows God that we trust Him and need Him. Once we know that we can share our true selves with Him in prayer without being punished, we can find peace within ourselves as He moves to bring peace in our situations.

He will bring peace to our crisis even if things haven't changed for the better.

Pay special attention to the truth that He will bring peace to our crisis even if things haven't changed for the better. We may still not see any positive change in our lives, but His peace will hold us until the change comes. We must see that the blessing in all of this is that we will stay in a peaceful state until our situation changes. This kind of peace is what is referred to as the "God kind of peace." It is a level of peace that most people never experience or understand. This is the peace that surpasses all understanding in **Philippians 4:7** that says,

And the peace of God, which transcends all understanding, will guard your hearts and your minds in Christ Jesus.

People who don't have a strong prayer life can't understand how you can be at peace, and your situation still seems to be unchanged. They can't understand how you can still be faithful in praising God, and your situation is still the same. They can't understand how you are so joyful and calm in the middle of all the negative things they see happening to you. They can't and won't ever understand because they have not reached the "still" level in prayer where you have not only found peace, but kept peace, while you watched God act on your behalf. What

When We Are "Still In Prayer," He Is Quick In Action

a blessing to know this truth! Well, it is there for you if you tap into it only through prayer.

Take a moment and write a *"confession prayer"* to God. Explain to Him that you want to be able to become more transparent and honest in your prayer life. Tell Him you trust Him with all your heart. Tell Him that you are glad to know that you will not be punished for not being perfect in your life. Tell Him that you trust Him with your deepest concerns and can't wait for Him to bring peace to you even before your situation changes.

_____

_____

_____

_____

_____

When We Are "Still In Prayer," He Is Quick In Action

We need to learn how to isolate ourselves from external circumstances and concerns while we are entering into the stillness of prayer.

We need to practice being still in our prayer time by learning how to isolate ourselves from external circumstances and concerns while we are entering into the stillness of prayer. Try this exercise, for example.

- First, make sure you are in a very quiet and isolated place where no one or nothing can disturb you.
- Next, get in a comfortable position where you can maintain a certain posture that makes it easy for you to prepare to talk with Lord. You may try sitting up straight in a chair. You may try reclining in a chair. You might even prefer standing. The point is to not choose a position in prayer that will not allow you to spend as much time connecting with God. Choose a position where you can be as comfortable as possible.
- After you have found a good position, try breathing in and out.
- Take some deep breaths in, and then exhale.
- As you inhale, think about the goodness of God and all He has done for you.

When We Are "Still In Prayer," He Is Quick In Action

- As you exhale, think about how much you love Him. Now, let's go a little deeper in the process of stillness.
- Inhale now, and think about the goodness of God.
- Then as you exhale, imagine your problem leaving you.
- Follow that up by inhaling again while thinking of His goodness again.
- Then exhale, picturing Him smiling at you and placing His hand on you — releasing peace on the top of your head that penetrates into your heart that you can now feel.
- Finally, just inhale deeply, and absorb the precious moment of peace. Drink it in, feel it, and try to taste it.
- Follow it up with one last very long exhale.

Try this entire exercise two times and afterwards write down how you felt after doing this.

_____
_____
_____
_____
_____

When We Are "Still In Prayer," He Is Quick In Action

Write down at least three things you inhaled in the exercise and three things you exhaled in the process.

I inhaled _____ the first time.
I exhaled _____ the first time.
I inhaled _____ the second time.
I exhaled _____ the second time.
I inhaled _____ the third time.
I exhaled _____ the third time.

Stillness is the key to becoming one with God where He will begin to act on your behalf to change you and your situation.

Remember, the key here is to make sure you are inhaling the goodness and blessings of God and exhaling the busyness and negative thoughts competing for your concentration in prayer. In addition to inhaling God in the exercise, you will soon find yourself in a realm of stillness. So, keep anticipating and watching for His presence. When you can reach a point in the inhaling and exhaling exercise that you can feel God, and totally feel connected with Him, you have reached the first level of *stillness*. When your thoughts become totally peaceful and heavenly, you have reached the second level of *stillness*. When you become aware of only the presence of God and nothing or no one else, you have reached the third level of *stillness*. Once you have achieved the third level of *stillness*, you are now ready to hear Him speak and watch Him move into action on your behalf. This is the fourth level of *stillness*.

Remember, *stillness* is the key to becoming one with God where He will begin to act on your behalf to change you and your situation. *Stillness*, allows action to be taken by God. A special word of caution must be given here: **We can't go to the highest level of stillness until we have achieved all the lower levels of stillness first.**

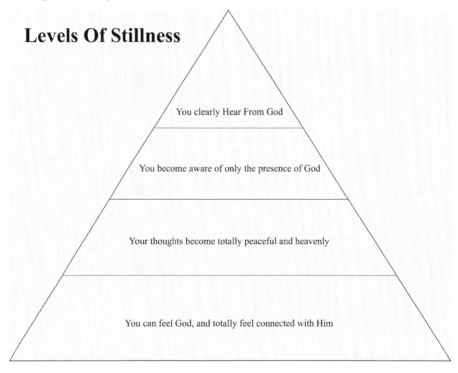

Chapter 4 Review and Exercise

1. It was Daniel's stillness in prayer that caused God's quick action.
2. If we don't stop our <u>busyness</u> in prayer, God can't start His <u>business</u> of answering us in prayer.
3. To hold peace means to receive it, feel it, and then retain it.
4. We must first receive and get the peace of God that can only come from God.
5. When we share our deepest feelings with God, our honesty shows Him we trust Him. Then, we can get peace with God.
6. He will bring peace to our crisis even if things haven't changed for the better.
7. We need to learn how to isolate ourselves from external circumstances and concerns while we are entering into the stillness of prayer.
8. *Stillness* is the key to becoming one with God where He will begin to act on your behalf to change you and your situation.
9. We can't go to the highest level of *stillness* until we have achieved all the lower levels of stillness first.

When We Are "Still In Prayer," He Is Quick In Action

Spiritual Exercise

1. Write down the key things you want God to reveal to you about being able to sense when change is taking place during your personal prayer time.

   _____
   _____
   _____
   _____
   _____

2. Write down the key things you learned in this chapter.

   _____
   _____
   _____
   _____
   _____

5

Praying From Your Heart, To God's Heart

"Not so, my lord," Hannah replied, "I am a woman who is deeply troubled. I have not been drinking wine or beer; I was pouring out my soul to the Lord."
1 Samuel 1:15

When we think about praying the perfect prayer, we may imagine lots of ways we've heard others pray. Often, we listen to others and settle on using their style and words in prayer as our own. Some of us have picked certain prayers from the Bible as the perfect prayer. And, many of us rely on the latest Christian authors to craft words that they label as the perfect prayer encouraging us to make these prayers our own. This chapter will challenge your thinking on what is the "perfect prayer."
Let's look at **1 Samuel 1:13-16**:

Hannah was praying in her heart, and her lips were moving but her voice was not heard. Eli thought she was drunk and said to her, "How long will you keep on getting drunk? Get rid of your wine." "Not so, my lord," Hannah replied, "I am a woman who is deeply troubled. I have not been drinking wine or beer; I was pouring out my soul to the Lord. Do not take your servant for a wicked woman; I have been praying here out of my great anguish and grief."

Look at the richness of these scriptures! There is so much here to learn and embrace. This chapter can only begin to show us how to pray the best prayer we can offer to God every time we come humbly to His throne of greatness. This chapter can only begin the process and lay the foundation. The rest is up to us to come to God uniquely, honestly, openly and totally connected to Him in prayer. Once we study the truths in this chapter and meditate on 1 Samuel 1:13-16, we should be able to begin to pray our best prayer to God. So let's take a peek at the richness of these scriptures.

Too many of us approach prayer trying to come to God based on how we have heard others pray.

Notice that verse 13 shows us that Hannah was praying in her heart. That is the key right there to connect with God uniquely and sincerely. She comes to God in the purest way she knows — not from her head; not from what she learned at church; not from what she heard someone else pray. She came to God in prayer and opened up her heart to Him. Too many of us approach prayer trying to come to God based on what we have heard others pray. We begin our prayers based on how others pray. We close our eyes, clasp our hands, sit up straight and start the prayer something like: "Our Father, who art in heaven, etc., etc., etc..." Sometimes we get really fancy and say things like: "Oh most Great High God Jehovah. You are the Lord of Lords and Master of all things. How great is your name and greatness? You are the one who makes the sun shine in the morning. You are the one who makes the moon shine at night. You are the one who makes the grass green and the flowers bloom." Then we get real comfortable and confident and will throw in a line like this: "You are the only God that can make a brown cow eat green grass and turn around to produce white milk."

We shouldn't continuously babble on and on in our prayers.

We go on and on and on and on. Then we wonder why after all of our eloquent and flamboyant salutations we still can't feel God or hear from Him. We wonder what else we could have done to move on God's heart to get Him to hear us and answer us. **Matthew 6:7-8** says:

And when you pray, do not keep on babbling like pagans, for they think they will be heard because of their many words. Do not be like them, for your Father knows what you need before you ask him.

The point here is that we shouldn't continue babbling on and on in our prayers. Matthew makes it clear that praying this way is unnecessary with God. Most people pray like this to God because they are trying to convince themselves that they are in a right relationship with Him. Some people pray like this because they are trying to convince God that they have reached a certain level of spirituality. And others pray this way because they are using flattery and false humility — fooling themselves to think that God can't see through their tricks. The word babbling comes from the Greek word, *battalogeō*, which means vain repetitions. In other words, the effort invested in long meaningless flattery and charm to God will not produce any more of a blessing in our lives at all.

We should pray on point, pray in truth and pray in time.

In fact, Matthew 6:7-8 goes on further to say that God doesn't want us to be like pagans or pray like them because it is simply a waste of time. God already knows what we want and need before we ask Him. We should come to prayer the following way. We should pray on point, pray in truth and pray in time.

A Strategy For Effective Prayer

Pray In Time
↓
Pray In Truth
↓
Pray On Point

Notice that every time we come to the part in prayer where we talk or initiate the conversation with God, we should pray in time. To pray in time means to be aware that God has allowed a certain window of time for us to connect with Him uniquely. Don't waste time with words that are empty and not full of power. These words cannot connect with God. And, God cannot meet our needs that He already knows we have, if we pray a useless prayer to Him.

We should pray from within ourselves with all the truth of ourselves.

We then must pray in truth. In other words, we must pray like Hannah prayed. She simply opened up her heart and prayed with all her might from within. She prayed from within herself with all the truth of herself. She wanted her truth to touch God's truth. God's truth is what He knows we should pray before we begin the prayer and what He expects us to pray knowing who we are.

Our truth should touch God's truth.

When our truth can touch God's truth, a connection is made and blessings flow from heaven. Touching our truth with God's truth is simply allowing our heart to touch God's heart. So, we don't have to waste a lot of time with empty words to God. If we speak to God in truth, the connection is quickly made and heaven opens.

The truth that we speak from our heart will connect with the truth of God. All we have to do is wait and watch for heaven to open.

Finally, once we are in truth, then we must pray on point. Praying on point means we must know the right words to pray to God. In other words, we must know the precise truth to speak to God about. Here is where a lot of people miss it. We must be at a point where we pray on point by not jumping and skipping around with words until we think we have found God's heart. We can't just keep talking and going on and on until we finally feel something that resembles God's anointing or His presence.

Many people miss the chance to pray on point because they jump and skip around so long in prayer that they miss the opportunity to see heaven open. So then, to pray on point is not a very difficult thing to do. We must just simply open up our hearts after centering ourselves on Him by closing out all anti-God thoughts, eliminating all external distractions and putting off all negative influences that are trying to affect us. When we become still and centered, our heart becomes engaged to God's heart. As a result, our heart then opens up, and we can speak truth to God. It is the truth that we speak from our heart that will connect with the truth of God. All we have to do now is wait and watch for heaven to open. Our heart reaching God's heart and our truth reaching God's truth opens up heaven like a key unlocks a door at our homes.

Practice for a moment the strategy for effective prayer: praying in time, praying in truth, and praying on point. Write down what you experienced after you complete this exercise.

_____

_____

_____

_____

_____

Prayer is the place where God will release His supply to meet our needs. He already knows what we need and when our needs should be met.

Again, prayer is not a place to come and waste valuable time convincing, pleading and politicking about what we want God to do for us. Prayer is also not the place where we come to try to get His attention about something we need because we feel He is so busy doing other things that He is not aware of that need. No! Prayer is the place where we can come and connect with Him for more than just having are needs met. We should expect our needs to be exceeded by God. The truth of this is found in **Ephesians 3:20**:

Now to him who is able to do immeasurably more than all we ask or imagine, according to his power that is at work within us.

How wonderful it is to know that He will exceed all of our needs. Here is a better way to look at this scripture. When we connect with God and are in time, in truth and on point, all the supply we need is released by God through prayer. Here's a thought. Prayer is the place where God will release His supply to meet our needs. He already knows what we need and when our needs should be met.

There is a specific time for how long heaven will be opened so that the supply God has for us can be released.

Now let's build on that with what we have learned in the previous chapters. When we feel a tugging in our hearts to come to prayer, the time has come for God to release His supply to us at our time of need. He then draws us to Him. As we center and quiet ourselves, by exhaling everything that is not of God and inhaling everything that is of God, we can open up ourselves. Then, we can see heaven open up and watch our supply being released to us by God. We know that there is a specific time for how long heaven will be opened so that the supply God has for us can be released. We should watch closely and wait until we see our supply from God come to us.

All we have to do is bring our questions to God in prayer, and the answers will be revealed to us every time as heaven opens up.

Look back at 1 Samuel 1:13. It says Hannah was praying in her heart. We must focus again on her intention about this prayer. She was praying in her heart. She wasn't trying to be cute with God. She wasn't trying to impress God. She wasn't trying to flatter Him. She simply had reached a point in her life where she wanted to see a change in her life and in her situation. She was hurt, down and full of doubt. She wanted a baby.

Why couldn't she have a child? All of the other women had children. How embarrassed she must have been to go into town and to worship service knowing that people were talking about her not being able to conceive. In biblical days, one of the worst things that could happen to a woman was that she could not have any children. It was considered a curse and a sign of personal weakness in the woman. She had tried so many times to get pregnant. She had been told by everyone that she would never have any children. So she found herself hurt, rejected by society and full of many questions for God.

Oh! There it is! She became full of many questions for God. All of a sudden she finds herself being drawn to prayer. Notice she is not praying at home. She is not calling every prayer line on Christian television. She is not asking everyone in the church to pray and touch and agree with her so that she can get pregnant. No! She is drawn to prayer. That drawing is so strong that she finds herself at the place of worship in front of the High Priest Eli.

She has to leave her place of doubt, trouble and fear and go where she feels the tugging leading her in her heart. Once she gets there, she doesn't care about what anyone says about her. She doesn't care about how anyone might look at her. She doesn't even care if she looks crazy or drunk. All she knows is that she is drawn to prayer. The power to pray is so strong on her that she must get to a place where she can pour her heart out to God. She then opens up her heart to God and lets Him know what is on her mind, and she waits to see heaven open.

What a blessing! She opens up her heart to God and He opens up His heart to her. As a result, her womb is opened up. Yes! Her womb is opened as heaven is opened as God's heart is opened. All of this happens because she first opened up her heart to God in truth. Let this be a lesson and example for all of us. If we really want to see the hand of God in our lives, we must make the effort to not be afraid to become truthful with Him whenever He chooses us to come to prayer in truth.

We should also not overlook the importance of our local church, which God has called us to be a part of. She has to get up, dress up and come up to her local place of worship and lay everything to God in front of everyone for them to see everything about her. It was her obedience to the drawing of the hand of God in prayer that brought her healing that day. Hannah walked in that place of worship determined not to leave the way she came in. She came in empty, she left full. She came in weak, she left with power. She came in hurt, she left with joy.

What a powerful resource we have when we accept the invitation of God for prayer. Just like the Jeopardy example in Chapter 3, we must accept the invitation to the game where the answers have already been prepared for us. Finally, all we have to do is bring our questions to God in prayer, and the answers will be revealed to us every time as heaven opens up.

Chapter 5 Review and Exercise

1. Too many of us approach prayer trying to come to God based on how we have heard others pray.
2. We shouldn't continuously babble on and on in our prayers.
3. We should pray on point, pray in truth and pray in time.
4. We should pray from within ourselves with all the truth of ourselves.
5. Our truth should touch God's truth.
6. The truth that we speak from our heart will connect with the truth of God. All we have to do is wait and watch for heaven to open.
7. Prayer is the place where God will release His supply to meet our needs. He already knows what we need and when our needs should be met.
8. There is a specific time for how long heaven will be opened so that the supply God has for us can be released.
9. All we have to do is bring our questions to God in prayer, and the answers will be revealed to us every time as heaven opens up.

Spiritual Exercise

1. Write down the key things you want God to reveal to you about being able to sense when change is taking place during your personal prayer time.

   _____
   _____
   _____
   _____
   _____

2. Write down the key things you learned in this chapter.

   _____
   _____
   _____
   _____
   _____

6

A Prayer That Only God Can Hear

…and her lips were moving but her voice was not heard. Eli thought she was drunk and said to her, "How long will you keep on getting drunk? Get rid of your wine."
1 Samuel 1:13-14

In the previous chapter, we learned about Hannah's perfect prayer to God. There is much more we can gain from Hannah's prayer. Let's take a deeper look at **1 Samuel 1:13-14** once more:

...and her lips were moving but her voice was not heard. Eli thought she was drunk and said to her, "How long will you keep on getting drunk? Get rid of your wine."

Pay close attention to this scripture and another prayer secret is revealed. The secret revealed here is that there is a realm or level of prayer that we can reach that will allow us to go beyond what we ourselves and others can hear and understand as we pray. In other words, there is a point in prayer where we will be so in tune with the Holy Spirit that we will look like we are doing natural, physical things, when in fact, we have transitioned into a supernatural realm. Watch this! Hannah was so focused and involved in her prayer, that Eli, the High Priest watched her move her lips but he couldn't hear anything. He even got frustrated at seeing her move her lips while no sound came out of her mouth. He thought she was drunk, and he sharply instructed her to stop drinking so much wine.

The Holy Spirit intercedes for us when we don't know what to say in our prayers.

This is one of the most beautiful things we can ever see happen in prayer. Notice that her lips moved, but the words she spoke couldn't be heard. Think about that. What could be the reason that her lips moved but the words couldn't be heard? Well, it is one of the biggest blessings God can provide for us in prayer. It is called intercession. That's right! This is a great example of the intercessory ministry of the Holy Spirit. Notice in **Romans 8:26-27** it says:

In the same way, the Spirit helps us in our weakness. We do not know what we ought to pray for, but the Spirit himself intercedes for us with groans that words cannot express. And he who searches our hearts knows the mind of the Spirit, because the Spirit intercedes for the saints in accordance with God's will.

Yes! The Holy Spirit intercedes for us when we don't know what to say in our prayers. It is when we don't know what to say in prayer, we can get in trouble and mess up our prayers. When our prayers are messed up, they aren't effective in getting God's attention.

The Holy Spirit will bring our prayers in line with God's will, so that our prayers are heard and answered by God only.

Let's look at the meaning of the word intercede. The word intercede has a three pronged meaning that must be dealt with in its entirety to completely understand the great work of the Holy Spirit. The word intercede means to:

a. Interpose, which means to intervene;

b. Put a barrier or obstacle between or in the way of something or someone; and

c. Bring influence, action or agreement to bear between parties, or on behalf of a party or person.

Please note that there is a progressive unfolding of the word, intercede. First, the Holy Spirit will intervene between us and the Father during prayer to listen to both sides to see what is being said. Second, the Holy Spirit will then block whatever parts of the prayer He doesn't want to be heard or understood by anyone who may be listening to the prayer. Finally, the Holy Spirit will bring our prayers in line with God's will, so that our prayers are heard and answered by God.

A Prayer That Only God Can Hear

> **The Holy Spirit Intercedes For Us In Prayer By:**
> 1. Intervening between us and the Father.
> 2. Listening to both sides to see what is being said.
> 3. Blocking whatever parts of prayer He doesn't want anyone else to hear.
> 4. Bringing our prayers in line with God's will, so that our prayers are heard and answered by God only.

The Holy Spirit steps in and makes our prayer perfect for God's purpose.

What a blessing that is! Now, let's go back to Hannah in 1 Samuel 1:13 where it says, **and her lips were moving but her voice was not heard.** Now pay close attention to this. Her lips are moving but the words can't be heard by Eli the Priest. Why? She is no longer speaking in prayer through her flesh. She is now praying from her heart with the assistance of the Holy Spirit. She has to be praying with the assistance of the Holy Spirit. She had come to the temple many times before and prayed but no answer came to her at all. Maybe she was so angry and bitter that she said the wrong things in prayer. Maybe she didn't know the correct things to say. Maybe she just was going through the motions and thought that just praying anything was good enough.

However, something great happens to her this time when she comes to the temple to pray. She encounters a realm of prayer where the Holy Spirit steps in and makes her prayer perfect for God's purpose. The Holy Spirit first looked at what had been placed in her heart to say by Christ. Next, when He saw that she was ready to pray from her heart to God's heart, He had to make sure that her words would not fall on the wrong ears and delay God's reply. The Holy Spirit then had to make sure that anyone eavesdropping on her prayers would not bring harm or ridicule to her. So, her words were not able to be heard by anyone but God the Father.

As she prayed, the Holy Spirit then made sure her words were shaped in the will of God the Father. As a result, her words reached heaven and it opened up her womb. What great news it is to know that the Holy Spirit will take our prayers and tune them in to a frequency that only God can hear what is in our heart. Eli the Priest couldn't even hear or understand her words because they were words from her heart to God and no one else.

The Holy Spirit will move sometimes on the hearts of others to relay God's answer to us.

Finally, through the guidance of the Holy Spirit, her prayers reached God as Eli tells her that what she has prayed for will come to pass. How interesting it is to know that Eli never heard what she was saying, but God moved on his heart to tell her that the prayer offered to God had been answered. Notice the beauty of this. God moved in her heart to speak from her heart. She then spoke from her heart to God's heart. Next, God moves on Eli the Priest's heart to speak His answer to her. Did you see the blessing in that? Hannah prayed from her heart but the Priest had to deliver the answer. Sometimes we can pray in our hearts with all our might and still not be able to hear what God is saying. The assurance we have of a heart-felt prayer is that sometimes God will send an answer to us through someone He chooses.

The work and ministry of the Holy Spirit was given by Christ to make sure all believers who pray to Him would pray a perfect prayer that lines up with the will of God.

Never forget the importance of a Pastor in your life. That is why church attendance is so important even today with us having the Holy Spirit permanently in our lives. After all the interceding the Holy Spirit will do for us, He will still move on the hearts of others to relay God's answer to us. He simply never stops until we get an answer. That is why when we go to church and the Pastor starts talking, everything he says sounds like it is intended just for us.

We may even say things like, "I thought he was only talking to me." Or, "That word was just what I needed." We may go on to add, "How did he know that I was going through that, or dealing with that?" We may even get to the point where we realize somewhere in the sermon that the message is speaking directly to our hearts. We'll say, "That message spoke to my heart." Guess what? It did. It was an answer to a prayer that came from your heart and reached God's heart. Now, you are receiving a blessing through your Pastor. Even in a time when people think the importance of a Pastor is small. Even in a time when everyone thinks as long as they have Christ, they have all they need. We have to be mindful of the fact that the work and ministry of the Holy Spirit was given by Christ to make sure all believers who pray to Him would pray a perfect prayer that lines up with the will of God. Look at **John 16:7:**

But I tell you the truth: It is for your good that I am going away. Unless I go away, the Counselor will not come to you; but if I go, I will send him to you.

> *The Holy Spirit's main job is to make known to us whatever Christ wants us to hear and receive what the Father has ordained for us to know.*

Now watch what Christ Jesus says about the blessing we will have when the Holy Spirit comes into our lives to help us in prayer. **John 16:13**-15 says,

But when he, the Spirit of truth, comes, he will guide you into all truth. He will not speak on his own; he will speak only what he hears, and he will tell you what is yet to come. He will bring glory to me by taking from what is mine and making it known to you. All that belongs to the Father is mine. That is why I said the Spirit will take from what is mine and make it known to you.

Yes! The Holy Spirit has a job. His main job is to make known to us whatever Christ wants us to hear and receive what the Father has ordained for us to know. Christ says the answer that the Father gives us will be made known to us in whatever fashion or form He chooses. However, the Holy Spirit has to make it happen. This is His major responsibility on this earth. So, if He has to speak through a Pastor to get the message to us, He will. If He has to speak through a prophet to get the message to us He will. Even if He has to speak through a donkey to get the message to us, He will. The message will get to us.

When it is time for God's purpose to be unfolded in our lives, the Holy Spirit will stand in the gap for us. He will speak for us and through us so that what is in our hearts is correctly expressed to the Father.

Examine **2 Peter 2:15-16** where it says,

They have left the straight way and wandered off to follow the way of Balaam son of Beor, who loved the wages of wickedness. But he was rebuked for his wrongdoing by a donkey — a beast without speech — who spoke with a man's voice and restrained the prophet's madness.

Yes! God used the Holy Spirit to speak through a donkey to save His prophet in order for His will to be done. If God can speak through a donkey, He can speak through a Pastor, prophet or any person. That's how much He loves us. And, that's how much we must be open to hear an answer from God's heart. What a blessing to know that when it is time for God's purpose to be unfolded in our lives, the Holy Spirit will stand in the gap for us. He will speak for us and through us so that what is in our hearts is correctly expressed to the Father.

Silent prayer keeps us focused on the truthfulness in our hearts that is trying to express itself externally without us messing it up.

Pray and ask the Holy Spirit to intercede with you and for you as you pray to God. Pray from your heart without speaking any words out of your mouth and record what you experience below.

_____

_____

_____

_____

_____

Silent prayer keeps us focused on the truthfulness in our hearts that is trying to express itself externally without us messing it up. That's right! There are times when we can, and will, mess up a perfect prayer that will fall short of God's ability to act according to His will concerning a situation or circumstance in our lives. In other words, sometimes our words get in the way of the truth that is trying to come out of us. So, we need help to make sure we pray a perfect prayer to unlock God's answers and purpose in our lives.

To be very honest, sometimes we don't even know what to say, and we will talk ourselves out of a blessing from God. We may even talk ourselves into a mess based on our inability to speak the right things in prayer. Notice again in **Romans 8:26** it says,

In the same way, the Spirit helps us in our weakness. We do not know what we ought to pray for, but the Spirit himself intercedes for us with groans that words cannot express.

Notice here that the Holy Spirit will help us in our areas of weakness concerning our inability sometimes to speak a perfect prayer. The Holy Spirit will literally move from within us and move on what Christ placed in us. The Holy Spirit will begin to make sure our words are truly expressed to the Father.

Let's look at **1 Samuel 1:15-16** once more:

"Not so, my lord," Hannah replied, "I am a woman who is deeply troubled. I have not been drinking wine or beer; I was pouring out my soul to the Lord. Do not take your servant for a wicked woman; I have been praying here out of my great anguish and grief."

She admits that she is at a very weak point in her life. She is deeply troubled and praying out of great anguish and grief. Anyone can easily see that she needs help, comfort and guidance.

It is when we approach prayer admitting to God that we are weak, He sends the Holy Spirit to help us.

Thank God that the Holy Spirit moved in Hannah's life. He will move in our lives the same way as well. In fact, it is her coming to the point where she realizes that she is weak, tired and not strong enough to bring a change in her life that the Holy Spirit moves on her and helps her in prayer. We need to approach prayer admitting to God that we are weak in our mind, heart and spirit when it comes to the things of life. It is when we take this humble approach to Him, He sends the Holy Spirit to help us.

When it comes to prayer, we should not be afraid to admit we are weak. It is in our admission of being weak that we will find strength in the Holy Spirit. Even the Apostle Paul says in **2 Corinthians 12:9**:

But he said to me, "My grace is sufficient for you, for my power is made perfect in weakness." Therefore I will boast all the more gladly about my weaknesses, so that Christ's power may rest on me.

Even Paul learned a valuable lesson in humility when it comes to praying to God. He learned that you must not be afraid to express to the Father your frustration, pain and grief when you pray. Are you frustrated about some things in life? Are you experiencing pain in your heart about something that happened to you? Are you grieving over something or someone you lost recently? If so, admit your true feelings to Him. Then, watch and see if His power won't come and rest on you.

Take a moment right now and pray in writing what you are frustrated about, hurting from and or grieving over.

_____

_____

_____

_____

_____

Chapter 6 Review and Exercise

1. The Holy Spirit intercedes for us when we don't know what to say in our prayers.
2. The Holy Spirit will bring our prayers in line with God's will, so that our prayers are heard and answered by God only.
3. The Holy Spirit steps in and makes our prayer perfect for God's purpose.
4. The Holy Spirit will move sometimes on the hearts of others to relay God's answer to us.
5. The work and ministry of the Holy Spirit was given by Christ to make sure all believers who pray to Him would pray a perfect prayer that lines up with the will of God.
6. The Holy Spirit's main job is to make known to us whatever Christ wants us to hear and receive what the Father has ordained for us to know.
7. When it is time for God's purpose to be unfolded in our lives, the Holy Spirit will stand in the gap for us. He will speak for us and through us so that what is in our hearts is correctly expressed to the Father.
8. Silent prayer keeps us focused on the truthfulness in our hearts that is trying to express itself externally without us messing it up.

9. It is when we approach prayer admitting to God that we are weak, He sends the Holy Spirit to help us.

A Prayer That Only God Can Hear

Spiritual Exercise

1. Write down the key things you want God to reveal to you about being able to sense when change is taking place during your personal prayer time.

   _____

   _____

   _____

   _____

   _____

2. Write down the key things you learned in this chapter.

   _____

   _____

   _____

   _____

   _____

7

God Will Speak To You, Through You

The word of the Lord came to me, saying,...
Jeremiah 1:4

Prayer is a way God can communicate whatever He wants to us whenever He wants to.

All of us believe in the power of prayer. There is no doubt that when we enter into prayer we have an assurance that God will hear the words we speak to Him. However, when it comes to hearing a reply back from Him, we are not so confident about when, how and where He will speak to us. Actually, this kind of approach to prayer is not the best strategy.

To approach prayer thinking we must first talk to God and then wait to hear from Him is not actually the way prayer has been designed by God. God designed prayer to be an open line of communication between Him and us. He may initiate the prayer, or we may initiate the prayer. The point is that we should understand that prayer is a way God can communicate whatever He wants to us whenever He wants to. Prayer is God's unique way of being involved in our lives whenever He needs to communicate His will to us. We can expect Him to lead us into prayer very often.

If we study scripture carefully, God initiated most of the prayers that mankind encountered. For example, look at **Jeremiah 1:4**:

The word of the Lord came to me, saying,...

Notice here that Jeremiah didn't approach God. God approached Jeremiah. The key point to note here is that Jeremiah recognized that it was the word of the Lord that was speaking to him. Not only did Jeremiah recognize that it was the word of the Lord, he knew it was the voice of the Lord because he states that, **The word of the Lord came to me, saying,...** He makes it clear that we must understand that the word not only came to him, but it "came saying." It is the "came saying" part that is powerful.

It was not a rhetorical word. It was not a reported word. It was a real time conversation with God where he could understand audibly what God was saying. Here we can see clearly the word of the Lord came to him speaking. That's right! The word of the Lord came to him speaking truth, purpose and power. God's word came to him so that he would know how God was going to use him in the future.

There are many other examples in the Bible showing how God initiated prayer with those He wanted to use to execute His will. We should stay alert and watchful of God to speak to us and through us with truth, purpose and power.

God Will Speak To You, Through You

God speaks very often through us in order to speak to us.

Some of the toughest questions people ask themselves when it comes to understanding prayer are:

- How do I recognize the voice of God?

- How will I know God is answering me?

- How can I be sure God is speaking to me?

- How can I be confident that God is speaking to me, and I am not talking to myself?

- How can I recognize the voice of God speaking to me the way Jeremiah did?

The answer is found in the fact that God can speak to us in many ways, but we must recognize when, how, where and through whom He may choose to speak. The very first and most important way we must recognize that He may choose to speak is through us. He desires to speak to us by speaking through us. We should not become uneasy about the fact that God prefers to speak directly through us as He is speaking directly to us. This is really the fastest, easiest and purest way He can speak to us. It is a direct line between us and Him where no one can tamper with the truthfulness of what He wants us to hear from Him.

God Will Speak To You, Through You

The truth that we must accept here is that God speaks very often through us in order to speak to us. However, most of us will confuse this with thinking that we are just talking to ourselves. We may think that we are just hearing our own voice in our heads. We may make the mistake of missing Him speak to us by saying things like, "something told me to," or "something said to me." We must make sure we don't miss His voice by thinking something or someone told us something in our heads when it was really God's voice we heard.

God will use the Holy Spirit to speak on His behalf in the form of your own voice.

Take a moment and think about the time when you approached an intersection. You pushed the accelerator down to the floor to speed through the traffic light. Then suddenly, you heard a voice in your head say, "Don't go through that light!" "Slow down and stop!" You stopped and another car coming from the opposite side of the intersection sped through the light. If you had not stopped, you would have been in an accident. You took a deep breath and said, "Something told me not to go through that light!" I am here to tell you that it was not "something" that spoke to you. It wasn't even "someone" who spoke to you. It was God that spoke through you to you! Yes!

God had to get that message to you very quickly or there would have been devastating results at that intersection you were about to cross. He spoke quickly and directly through you to protect you. There was not enough time for someone else to tell you to slow down. It would have been too late. There had to be an immediate line of communication where there was no doubt on your part that God was speaking. God used the Holy Spirit to speak on His behalf in the form of your own voice to save you from being in an accident.

Scripture supports this truth in **2 Samuel 23:2:**

The Spirit of the Lord spoke through me; his word was on my tongue.

Do you see it? Samuel shows us that the Lord spoke through David and instructed him on what to say. In other words, David is speaking in his own voice, but it is God who is directing what he says. We must stop saying, "something told me." We must now say, "The Holy Spirit told me," or "God told me."

Let's take another look at **Psalms 45:1**:

My heart is stirred by a noble theme as I recite my verses for the king; my tongue is the pen of a skillful writer.

Here we see David showing us that his tongue was being directed by the mouth of God. In other words, whatever God instructs his tongue to say, David will say. Our tongues should be under the authority of God and available to be used by Him however He wants to use our tongues. This is what happens when someone prophesies to us. Even though they are speaking in their own voice, it is God speaking through them to us.

You will begin to experience a peaceful and Godly presence in the midst of the conversation as God begins to speak to you during prayer.

Take a moment now. Just center, and quiet yourself. Listen in your head to hear your voice as God begins to speak through you, to you. Here is a little help. When you start this exercise, you may hear silly, stupid, even anti-Christ statements. You may even hear evil things. Immediately count what you hear as not the voice of God. Here is where evil thoughts will try to enter your mind. Evil thoughts are always in competition with the voice of God. Beware that evil thoughts will try to get you off track when it comes to hearing directly from God. Always remember that there is a way to begin to tell when God is speaking through you and to you. You will begin to experience a peaceful and Godly presence in the midst of the conversation. Go ahead and begin this exercise. Write down what you hear God saying to you.

_____
_____
_____
_____
_____

Whenever God is speaking through us and the message is for us, we are prophesying to ourselves.

If we can accept the truth that a prophet can speak in his own voice directly from God to us, we should easily grasp the truth that we can speak in our own voice as God is directly speaking through us. If we believe a prophecy can come to us through someone else, we should also believe that we can prophesy to ourselves as well. That's right! We should not be afraid to prophesy to ourselves. Whenever God is speaking through us, and the message is for us, we are prophesying to ourselves. What a blessing this is to know! You may think that you are just speaking in your head. You may think that you are just talking to yourself. You may even think that your mind is speaking to you. No! When it comes to the things of God and the fruit of the Spirit, it is God speaking to you and through you.

We can't create a prophecy from within ourselves on our own.

An important point is that we can't create a prophecy from within ourselves on our own. We shouldn't say that the voice we heard originated in our own minds. Did you get that? God has even wired us to not be able to fool ourselves. We couldn't even trick ourselves into speaking a prophecy if we tried. To prove this truth, look at **2 Peter 1:21**:

For prophecy never had its origin in the will of man, but men spoke from God as they were carried along by the Holy Spirit.

Do you see it? Did you grasp that truth? The scripture plainly and clearly says that prophecy **NEVER** had its **ORIGIN** in the **WILL** of **MAN**. It goes on to say that when a man would speak, he did not speak on his own or from his mind. Man spoke from God. In other words, the message originated from God as they were under the direction of the Holy Spirit. So go ahead, prophesy to yourself based on what you hear God saying to you.

Listen to what He has to say about your life! Listen to what He has to say about your finances! Listen to what He has to say about your job, marriage, children, home and church. Listen, and let Him speak His thoughts through you. Be assured that when His thoughts are expressed through you, they will come to pass. Remember, this is not something that originated from you. It originated from God. Therefore, if God has said it, it is done in the name of Christ Jesus. What a blessing!

Words of God must originate from Him, not us.

Again, the key truth here is to remember that the words of God must originate from Him, not us. How then do we make sure of that? How do we make sure that we are not forcing our will into a prayer? The answer is we must surrender our will to God every single time we enter prayer. Surrendering our will to conform to God's will is the ultimate form of humility that we can show to our heavenly Father. **Ephesians 5:17** says:

Therefore do not be foolish, but understand what the Lord's will is.

This is a key truth for us to be able to make sure our prayers get their life and strength from God. We must make sure that we understand what the Lord's will is concerning certain issues in our lives. By hearing Him speak to us and through us, we may find out that we are facing some challenges in our lives that had nothing to do with us falling short of His grace or anything that we did wrong. It may be God's will to allow us to experience something challenging in order to get to the blessing He has for us.

There is comfort in knowing that God will prophesy through us and to us by showing us challenging things that are destined to come into our lives.

Most people don't like this kind of talk, but there are times we have to take a more challenging path than we would like to take in order for certain parts of our character, demeanor and attitude to be shaped and conformed into the image of Christ.

We must never forget one of the greatest secrets in life. That secret is this. It is not getting what you want that is important, but wanting it and being able to hold on to it after you get it. This is a great secret that we must never forget. The ability to hold on to something and have peace after we obtain it is the key to our happiness on earth. We must learn that getting things are most often the easiest part. It is keeping them without losing our minds, peace and tranquility that is the more challenging part. That is why God sometimes chooses to take us through a more challenging path on our way to achieving His purpose in our lives.

Now, would you rather go through a challenging time unexpectedly? Or would you rather know what challenges will come your way and be prepared for them knowing that Christ is with you to bring you peace in the process of fulfilling God's purpose? There is comfort in knowing that God will prophesy through us and to us by showing us challenging things that are destined to come into our lives. But, He will bring us peace and patience to endure those challenges. And, we become better off after going through that process. There is no better display of this than what is written in **2 Corinthians 4:16-18**:

Therefore we do not lose heart. Though outwardly we are wasting away, yet inwardly we are being renewed day by day. For our light and momentary troubles are achieving for us an eternal glory that far outweighs them all. So we fix our eyes not on what is seen, but on what is unseen. For what is seen is temporary, but what is unseen is eternal.

We are inwardly renewed every day through prayer where God will let us know what to expect and how to deal with it. We might be praying one day, and God speaks through us and to us and says, "Look at 2 Corinthians 4:16-18." He may go on to say that this scripture is for us to be able to handle unforeseen circumstances in the next four weeks. If we casually read over it and immediately become turned off by it, we will miss the blessing in the passage that God wants us to get. Go ahead and look at 2 Corinthians 4:16-18 again. After looking at it again, you may be saying to yourself, "What is the blessing for me in this scripture?" You may even go on to say to yourself, "I sure don't see any blessing in this scripture." Well, I am here to tell you this passage of scripture is loaded with blessings.

Now watch this powerful insight. Look at what trouble has been designed to do. If you continue to look at the scripture, I promise that it will begin to open up to you just like heaven opened for Christ in Luke 3:21. Literally, when scripture opens up to you, heaven is opening up as well. Again, scripture opens up because heaven opens up. Why? Because the voice of God will begin to speak to you, through you! Just as heaven opened and the voice of God from heaven spoke to Jesus, the same thing will happen as we meditate on this passage of scripture.

Let's take a look at **2 Corinthians 4:16-18** again where it says:

Therefore we do not lose heart. Though outwardly we are wasting away, yet inwardly we are being renewed day by

day. For our light and momentary troubles are achieving for us an eternal glory that far outweighs them all. So we fix our eyes not on what is seen, but on what is unseen. For what is seen is temporary, but what is unseen is eternal.

We commonly view trouble as a terrible thing. But, look at what the Bible says about troubles. The scripture says troubles are light and momentary. Did you get this? Do you see it? Troubles are viewed as light by God. In other words, troubles are something that God designed for us to be able to carry. We can carry all our troubles easily as long as we present them to Christ Jesus. He converts them to become a lighter burden for us in the natural. They become very light to us as we share our load with Him.

Matthew 11:29-30 supports this truth as it says,

Take my yoke upon you and learn from me, for I am gentle and humble in heart, and you will find rest for your souls. For my yoke is easy and my burden is light.

Many people make the mistake of thinking that if they can just carry their burdens to the Lord and leave them there, all will be okay. We may even think that we won't have to deal with that particular trouble anymore. This kind of thinking is wrong thinking. The truth is that when we carry our troubles or burdens to the Lord, our troubles may not always immediately leave us. However, there is joy in knowing that Christ will become one with us or yoked to us, and He will help us carry the load of our burdens. Christ will share the load of our burdens until God has allowed trouble to run its course in our lives. Now you may be saying, "What good are troubles to me?" Well, they are designed to be momentary. Troubles are not supposed to last always. Troubles are only momentary. **2 Corinthians 4:17** says,

For our light and momentary troubles are achieving for us an eternal glory that far outweighs them all.

Now that we see that, let's focus on the reason and purpose of troubles in our lives. Troubles are designed to achieve for us a greater glory in Christ. Troubles have been designed by God to help us achieve a greater glory in Him. Look at 2 Corinthians 4:17 above. Knowing this truth, we should welcome a direct word from God that shows us challenging times ahead. It should be okay that things are going to be a little difficult. It should be okay about all these things as long as we know we have the presence and power of Christ in our lives to not just overcome, but grow from such challenging times. What a blessing from God.

What a blessing it is when we are able to see the unseen realities of the goodness of God and the fruit of the Holy Spirit!

So, why then do we always get nervous, upset and scared when we are faced with these challenges? It is because we forget the word that came to us in prayer saying, "So we fix our eyes not on what is seen, but on what is unseen. For what is seen is temporary, but what is unseen is eternal," that is found in 2 Corinthians 4:18. How can we get to this point? How can we stay focused on our blessing in the midst of a storm? We have to pray with our eyes open, look up to heaven and train ourselves to be able to see unseen things that are eternal and not look at seen things that are temporary.

What a blessing it is when we are able to see the unseen realities of the goodness of God and the fruit of the Holy Spirit! Even Christ Jesus, enduring all the ridicule and evil things happening to Him as He was nailed to the cross, did not come down because He saw something no one else could see but Him. That one thing He saw that kept Him through His pain, hurt and disappointment, was the joy that was set before Him. **Hebrews 12:2** shows this truth as it says,

Let us fix our eyes on Jesus, the author and perfecter of our faith, who for the joy set before him endured the cross,

scorning its shame, and sat down at the right hand of the throne of God.

Yes! Joy was set before Him before He even got up on the cross. Joy was there waiting on Him before they even stretched Him up there. It was joy that placed Him there, and joy that kept Him up there. What was this joy He knew about? It was Him knowing that we would have eternal life now because we would always believe in Him and what He had done for us. We would know that He died for our sins and we would have everlasting life by committing our lives to Him and His cause. What a blessing that is for us to know! JOY TO THE WORLD! THE LORD HAS COME! LET EARTH REDEEM HER KING!

Chapter 7 Review and Exercise

1. Prayer is a way God can communicate whatever He wants to us whenever He wants to.
2. God speaks very often through us in order to speak to us.
3. God will use the Holy Spirit to speak on His behalf in the form of your own voice.
4. You will begin to experience a peaceful and Godly presence in the midst of the conversation as God begins to speak to you during prayer.
5. Whenever God is speaking through us and the message is for us, we are prophesying to ourselves.
6. We can't create a prophecy from within ourselves on our own.
7. Words of God must originate from Him, not us.
8. There is comfort in knowing that God will prophesy through us and to us by showing us challenging things that are destined to come into our lives.
9. What a blessing it is when we are able to see the unseen realities of the goodness of God and the fruit of the Holy Spirit!

God Will Speak To You, Through You

Spiritual Exercise

1. Write down the key things you want God to reveal to you about knowing how and when He speaks through you during your personal prayer time.

   _____

   _____

   _____

   _____

   _____

2. Write down the key things you learned in this chapter.

   _____

   _____

   _____

   _____

   _____

8

Meditate Until You See Your Blessing

My eyes stay open through the watches of the night, that I may meditate on your promises.

Psalms 119:148

There will be times when God's answer to our prayers is in the form of a promise.

We know by now that God answers our prayers. He will answer us because He cares for us and loves us. However, we need to understand that when He answers us, it could be something He wants us to know now about a future time. How often have you prayed to God and heard Him answer in the form of a promise? In other words, are there times when God speaks to you and tells you that He will do something, but that something will occur at a later date? Most of us love when God speaks to us, but we don't like when His answers come in the form of a promise.

One of the reasons we are not too happy about promises is because we have to wait to see them manifest in our lives. We won't see them happen immediately, but rest assured, they will come to pass in our lives. Maybe if we understood the power behind a promise from God, we would be more willing to wait on His blessings to manifest in our lives at the time He ordained them occur.

The promise is not made to us, it is made for us. In other words, God speaks to His words, and they must do what He says.

The word promise is derived from the Greek word, *epangelia*, which means to summons. Now, to really get a good understanding of the word promise, we must learn that the definition of the word summons means that an authoritative call or notice has been given by someone for a specific purpose, or that someone is required to appear at a specific place for a particular purpose or duty. Let's think about this for a minute. This means that when God speaks to us and says He is going to do something, a promise has been spoken. Please pay special attention that the promise is not made to us, it is made for us. In other words, God speaks to His words, and they must do what He says. He literally commissions or summons His word to do something for Him, and it must do what it has been summoned to do.

Let's take a look at **Isaiah 55:9-11** where it says,

As the heavens are higher than the earth, so are my ways higher than your ways and my thoughts than your thoughts. As the rain and the snow come down from heaven, and do not return to it without watering the earth and making it bud

and flourish, so that it yields seed for the sower and bread for the eater, so is my word that goes out from my mouth: It will not return to me empty, but will accomplish what I desire and achieve the purpose for which I sent it.

Again, we can see clearly now how God summons His word to appear at certain place, expects His word to perform and anticipates His word returning to Him having achieved His purpose for which the word was sent. This key point is outstanding for you and me to know. And, it helps us rest in prayer knowing that God will do exactly what He promised for us. We just need to have the assurance that what He said will happen at the appointed time.

When we receive an answer from God in prayer, the hardest part for us is to wait with the assurance and confidence that what He said will be done.

When we receive an answer from God in prayer, the hardest part for us is to wait with the assurance and confidence that what He said will be done. Now, however, there is hope for us all. Scripture helps us have peace and gives us the ability to wait with patience and confidence. By focusing on scripture, we are able to meditate on what He has promised. The truth revealed here allows us to know that He has developed a truth principle called, "meditation." Meditation allows us to maintain peace, assurance and patience as we wait on His promises to show up in our lives.

It is only through the truth principle of meditation that a promise spoken by God can manifest to us.

Look at **Psalms 119:148** where it says,

My eyes stay open through the watches of the night, that I may meditate on your promises.

It is only through the truth principle of meditation that a promise spoken by God can manifest to us. The psalmist says that he meditates throughout the nights at assigned times to make sure that he stays focused on all the promises that God has spoken to him. He wants to do his part to make sure that what God has promised him will come to him. The key point for us to learn here and never forget is that meditation releases the promises of God to us.

If you ask someone what meditation means, he or she will most likely begin to describe a person sitting in a position with his or her legs folded, hands opened, eyes closed and with humming sounds coming out of their mouths. While in this position, most people who meditate are just hammering away at anything they can think of or what comes to their minds. However, scripture clearly defines for us what meditation is and how to do it.

Our meditation should be focused on the law of the Lord.

Scripture says in **Psalms 1:2:**

But his delight is in the law of the Lord, and on his law he meditates day and night.

Here we can see that our meditation should be focused on the law of the Lord. The law of the Lord is whatever God has summoned or promised for us. Please note that scripture says we are now to direct our focus on the law of the Lord, or words spoken by the Lord. Now, let's define meditation in a very deep level to grasp this truth. The Hebrew word meditate comes from Strong's number 7878. It is pronounced, *see'-akh*. It is through this deep study of the *Theological Wordbook of the Old Testament* number 2255 that we can accurately define meditate to mean, "to go over a matter in one's mind," "repent" and "rehearse."

Meditate Until You See Your Blessing

Stages of Meditation
Ponder God's Promises In Our Minds
↓
Repent By Changing Our Minds
↓
Rehearse What God Said He Would Do

Meditation is more of a progressive response to a promise from release stress God than an isolated exercise that we do to just feel better or.

So, meditation is more of a progressive response to a promise from God than an isolated exercise that we do to just feel better or release stress. First, we must go over in our mind's what God has said He will do. We literally have to ponder or deeply think about what He said. Deeply thinking about what God said means we must go over that particular promise in our minds. We must always remember that if our minds can't comprehend and accept what God has promised, nothing can show up for us. Our minds must focus on His promises and realize that they are for the fulfilling of God's purpose through our lives.

> *It is when we ponder God's perfect promises in our minds that we remove all doubt and confusion about what He said He will do.*

We must further know that God's promises spoken to us will always place us in His perfect will. It is when we ponder God's perfect promises in our minds that we remove all doubt and confusion about what He said He will do. We can then rest assured that we are in His perfect will. **Romans 12:2** says,

Do not conform any longer to the pattern of this world, but be transformed by the renewing of your mind. Then you will be able to test and approve what God's will is—his good, pleasing and perfect will.

Meditating on God's promises renews our minds to the things God wants to do through us and give to us. Renewing literally means to restore or replenish us to a place of purpose in God. It is when we can tap into the purposes of God, we are automatically renewed in our strength, confidence and hope. We begin to operate in a more vigorous and energetic manner as we do our daily tasks knowing that we are productive in fulfilling God's purpose for our lives. Let's not forget that the key here is to make sure we renew our minds on the promises of God by thoroughly focusing on what He said He wants to do through us.

Once our minds have been renewed, we must change the way we think about our new direction.

The next stage of meditation is the repenting stage. The word repent means to change one's mind. So, once our minds have been renewed, we must change the way we think about our new direction. We can't go back to our old way of thinking once we have been given a newness of thought. This means that we will be tempted to fall into doubt, fear and guilt as we begin to execute the promises of God. Issues or circumstances may come to us and we will be tempted to revert to our old way of thinking on how to deal with these issues.

We must know that we are a new creation in Christ when our minds have been renewed through meditation. We must fight off the urge to use our old ways of solving problems. We must allow our renewed mind to show us God's way of dealing with unforeseen circumstances. So, it is the repenting or changing from the way we did things that becomes difficult for us. It is hard to try a new way for solving old problems. However, when we repent and lean on God's newness, which has been placed in our minds, we will experience positive results as we progress in fulfilling His purpose in our lives.

This truth is illustrated in **Ephesians 4:22-24** where it says,

You were taught, with regard to your former way of life, to put off your old self, which is being corrupted by its deceitful desires; to be made new in the attitude of your minds; and to put on the new self, created to be like God in true righteousness and holiness.

We can see the importance of having a new attitude in our minds, which can only come through proper meditation in prayer.

After pondering God's word and repenting, we must rehearse His promises to prepare us for what is to come.

Finally, after pondering God's word and repenting, we must rehearse His promises to prepare us for what is to come.

Again, **Psalms 119:148** says,

My eyes stay open through the watches of the night, that I may meditate on your promises.

Next, look at **Psalms 45:1** where it says,

My heart is stirred by a noble theme as I recite my verses for the king; my tongue is the pen of a skillful writer.

From these two scriptures, we are to make sure that we continue the practice of meditation even through the night. We are to recite the theme of what God has promised us continuously. When we think of the word rehearse, we must not miss the power that is there for us to grasp. When an actor is given a particular role by a director to play in a movie, the actor is presented with a script. The director knows the beginning and end of the movie. The director designed the movie and knows the overall theme that he or she wants to come forward in the movie. The actor must recite or rehearse lines from the script in the movie to know what to say at the right time so that the movie will be portrayed as planned. It is the rehearsal of the lines by the actor that allows the movie to be successful as everyone will know the part and know what is going to happen at every stage of the movie.

As much as the director knows the theme of the movie, the script of the movie and the outcome of the movie, the movie will not be successful if the actors don't rehearse their lines. It is the same way for us in life. The Holy Spirit is the director of our lives, and God the Father has written a script for us to follow. That script is revealed to us in the words of Christ Jesus through the Holy Spirit for us to recite. As we recite and rehearse those words or promises from God, our lives take on a theme of victory, success and purpose.

However, special care must be taken to remember that we are reciting God's promises so that our minds will continuously be engaged with the reality of what He said will come to pass. Our repeating of what God promised will not hurry Him in delivering to us what He said. Our repeating of God's promises shows God our trust and hope in Him. When God sees our hope and trust in Him as we meditate on His promises, He then knows that we have faith in Him to do what He said He will do.

Again, it is the meditation process of prayer where we ponder on what He said in our minds, repent from our old way of thinking and rehearse what we know will happen. It is these things that we do in meditation that will bring His promises to life for us.

Practice the first stage of meditation by focusing your mind on what God has promised to you. Think deeply about it. Turn it over in your mind and write your thoughts below.

_____
_____
_____
_____
_____

Meditate Until You See Your Blessing

Go to the second stage of meditation where you repent, or change from your old way of thinking in your mind about how you will approach the undertaking of fulfilling the part you must play in seeing God's promises come to fruition in your life. In other words, write down how you will:

- Deal with unforeseen circumstances concerning His promises.
- Take a new approach to letting Him work through you in fulfilling His promises.
- Surrender your old way of doing things while you begin to walk in a new way of trusting Him to move through you to fulfill His will in your life.

_____
_____
_____
_____
_____

Meditate Until You See Your Blessing

Finally, in the last stage of meditation write down the promises you are to rehearse during the day and night as they come to your remembrance.

_____
_____
_____
_____
_____

Chapter 8 Review and Exercise

1. There will be times when God's answer to our prayers is in the form of a promise.
2. The promise is not made to us, it is made for us. In other words, God speaks to His words, and they must do what He says.
3. When we receive an answer from God in prayer, the hardest part for us is to wait with the assurance and confidence that what He said will be done.
4. It is only through the truth principle of meditation that a promise spoken by God can manifest to us.
5. Our meditation should be focused on the law of the Lord.
6. Meditation is more of a progressive response to a promise from God than an isolated exercise that we do to just feel better or release stress.
7. It is when we ponder God's perfect promises in our minds that we remove all doubt and confusion about what He said He will do.
8. Once our minds have been renewed, we must change the way we think about our new direction.
9. After pondering God's word and repenting, we must rehearse His promises to prepare us for what is to come.

Spiritual Exercise

1. Write down the key things you want God to reveal to you about being able to sense when change is taking place during your personal prayer time.

   _____
   _____
   _____
   _____
   _____

2. Write down the key things you learned in this chapter.

   _____
   _____
   _____
   _____
   _____

9

Get Ready To Open Heaven

After you have read this book, you will have reached a new level of prayer where heaven will open up for you again and again. There are many truths you have learned and exercises you have completed. Now, we must put all the pieces together.

Prayer can become an overwhelming experience unless the way you approach prayer is structured properly. Prayer should be a simple act of communication between you and God with the help of Jesus and the Holy Spirit. Let's summarize the truths in each chapter and come up with a strategy so that your prayers can cause heaven to open up every time you pray.

The Eight Truths of Prayer That Open Heaven

Truth #1: *As we pray, heaven opens up for us.*

Truth #2: *We should expect change to occur within us immediately as we are praying.*

Truth #3: *God answers our prayers before we pray.*

Truth #4: *We must reach a level of stillness in prayer in order for God to act on our behalf.*

Truth #5: *When we pray from our hearts, we reach God's heart.*

Truth #6: *The Holy Spirit intercedes for us to allow us the opportunity to be able to pray the perfect prayer that only our Father can hear.*

Truth #7: *God speaks to us, through us.*

Truth #8: *The promises of God are revealed to us through meditation.*

Truth # 1: *As we pray, heaven opens up for us.* We must never forget this truth. We must picture heaven opening up as we look at the ceiling of our homes. We must picture heaven opening up as we look toward the sky. If we keep looking up, heaven will eventually open. Remember the cube exercise? We looked at the cube and, as we looked at the cube, it began to rotate and move to show different openings. That is the same way heaven opens for us. Heaven opens as we stare and focus on the clouds and sky above us. It literally will open up for us right in front of our eyes.

Truth # 2: *We should expect change to occur within us immediately.* That's right. We should expect inward and outward changes to occur in the process of the actual prayer we are bringing forward. We should expect our disposition to change first. In other words, our mood and emotions should positively change while we are in the prayer process. Next, we should expect an outward change to occur for us as well. If Jesus' clothes can change, then we should know that everything that tries to attach itself or come into contact with us will change as well.

Don't forget that as we are praying, we should experience "The Nine Prayer Points of Completeness." The Nine Prayer Points of Completeness are stages we should experience as change begins to take place during our prayer. The Nine Prayer Points of Completeness start with us experiencing God's presence. God's presence is felt in our natural bodies. Once His presence is felt in our natural bodies, it changes our mental and emotional state. Our emotional state is the critical point where we then develop a positive outlook on life. After we have developed a positive outlook on life, our mood becomes positive.

Our mood then defines our character or the way people remember who we are based on how we act. Finally, our character creates the type of attitude that we display to everyone we encounter. Our attitudes also determine how we approach and handle challenges we may face as well.

Truth # 3: *God answers our prayers before we pray.* In fact, God has prepared all the answers for us before we pray. He then moves on us to have a desire to pray so that we will ask Him the right questions that releases the answers God will reveal to us at our time of need. The questions that we ask in our prayers are designed by the Father to allow His answers to take care of whatever decisions, issues or circumstances we may face. Prayer is the place where God has chosen for His answers to be revealed to us through the questions we ask Him.

Truth # 4: *We must reach a level of stillness in prayer in order for God to act on our behalf.* Too often we are busy, nervous and rushed when it comes to prayer. It is in our stillness that we become centered on God and His goodness. We must strive to reach the deepest level of stillness when we pray to God. There are four levels of stillness that we must understand how to reach.

Stillness is entered by learning and practicing inhaling and exhaling exercises. When you can reach a point in the inhaling and exhaling exercise that you can feel God, and totally feel connected with Him, you have reached the first level of *stillness*. When your thoughts become totally peaceful and heavenly, you have reached the second level of *stillness*. When you become aware of only the presence of God and nothing or no one else, you have reached the third level of *stillness*. Once you have achieved the third level of *stillness*, you are now ready to hear Him speak and watch Him move into action on your behalf. This is the fourth and deepest level of *stillness*.

Truth # 5: ***When we pray from our hearts, we reach God's heart.*** What a beautiful truth to know. It is our heart-felt prayers that move on God's heart, and He gives us His attention. The beauty of praying with our heart lies in the fact that it keeps us from babbling with meaningless and aimless words. A heart-led prayer allows us to pray in time, pray in truth and pray on point.

To *pray in time* means to be aware of the truth that God has allowed a certain window of time for us to connect with Him uniquely. We then must *pray in truth*. We must simply open up our hearts and pray with all our might from within ourselves. If we speak to God in truth, the connection is quickly made and heaven opens. *Praying on point* means we must know the right words to pray to God. In other words, we must know the precise truth to speak to God about. We *pray on point* when we don't jump and skip around with words as we pray to God. When we become *still* and *centered*, our heart becomes engaged to God's heart. As a result, our heart then opens up, and we can speak truthfully to God.

Truth # 6: *The Holy Spirit intercedes for us to allow us the opportunity to be able to pray the perfect prayer that only our Father can hear.* The Holy Spirit intercedes for us when we don't know what to say in our prayers. The Holy Spirit will intervene between us and the Father during prayer to listen to both sides to see what is being said. The Holy Spirit will then block the parts of the prayer from anyone who shouldn't hear or understand what is said between you and God. Finally, the Holy Spirit will bring our prayers in line with God's will, so that our prayers are heard and answered by God only.

Truth # 7: *God speaks to us, through us.* **2 Samuel 23:2 says, The Spirit of the Lord spoke through me; his word was on my tongue.** Samuel shows us that the Lord can speak through us and instruct us on what to say. In other words, when God is speaking to us, we may be speaking in our own voice but it is God who is directing what we say. He is speaking through us, not just to us. When we hear a peaceful, Godly voice in our head talking, we must not say, "Something told me." We must now say, "The Holy Spirit told me," or "God told me." Finally, our tongues should be under the authority of God and opened to be used by Him however He wants to. This is what happens when someone prophesies to us. They are speaking in their voice, but it is God speaking through them to us.

Truth # 8: *The promises of God are revealed to us through meditation.* Meditation is more of a progressive response to a promise from God than an isolated exercise that we do to just feel better or release stress. First, we must go over in our minds what God has said He will do. We literally have to ponder or deeply think about what He said. Deeply thinking about what God has said means we must go over that particular promise in our minds.

We must always remember that if our minds can't comprehend and accept what God has promised, nothing can materialize for us. Our minds must focus on His promises and realize that these promises are for the fulfilling of God's purpose through our lives. We must further know that God's promises spoken to us will always place us in His perfect will. It is when we ponder God's perfect promises in our minds, we remove all doubt and confusion about what He said He will do.

How To Get Heaven To Open When We Pray

Now that we know the eight truths of prayer that will open up heaven for us, how do we put it all together? Here are the steps we should take to ensure that heaven will open for us when we pray.

Step 1: Mentally believe and picture heaven opening up to you. As you pray, it actually will. Before we begin our prayer, we must mentally imagine heaven opening up. As we imagine this mentally, it will actually happen.

Step 2: As we pray, we should expect change to occur immediately. Once we begin to pray and are in the act of praying, we should expect an inward and outward change to occur in the process of our prayer. If you don't feel a change in your demeanor, keep trying until it happens.

Step 3: As you feel drawn to prayer, God is ready to reveal answers to you about circumstances you face. We must know that it is really God who is drawing us to prayer. He has answers for us that He wants to reveal to us through prayer.

Step 4: You must still yourself in order to be able to connect and hear from God. We must reach the deepest level of *stillness* where we will be able to connect with God and get ready to hear from Him.

Step 5: We can confidently pray from our heart to God's heart as heaven opens up. Once we connect with God, it is then that our hearts will reach God's heart. God will then become attentive to our prayers and move on our behalf.

Step 6: The Holy Spirit will intercede for us and help us pray the perfect prayer every time. The Holy Spirit will begin to intercede for us as we commune with God. He will make us pray the perfect prayer to God every time. As we approach this part of prayer we must be confident that we can pray the perfect prayer from our heart as the Holy Spirit will assist us in saying the right things to God.

Step 7: We should get ready to hear God speak to us, through us. We can expect God to begin to answer us. He will begin to talk to us and direct us.

Step 8: He may speak in the form of a promise that can only be manifested through meditation. We must understand that sometimes He will answer us in the form of a promise. A promise from God is a guarantee that He will do something through us for the purpose He has for our lives. Promises are different from answers in that they are something commissioned to happen at a specific time. We must meditate on what He promises us until His promises appear at His appointed time.

When we can grasp these steps based on the eight truths that open heaven and practice them in our actual prayer time, we will see heaven open and deliver the good things of God.

Chapter 9 Spiritual Exercises

1. Write down the eight truths of prayer that open heaven.

_____
_____
_____
_____
_____
_____
_____
_____

2. Next, write down the eight steps we must go through in prayer in order to get heaven to open.

_____
_____
_____
_____
_____
_____
_____
_____

3. Finally, write down a heart-felt prayer to God asking Him to move on your heart to master all truths taught in this book so that you can have a more powerful prayer life.

_____

_____

_____

_____

_____

_____

Epilogue

One of the surest ways to experience prayers that will open heaven for you is to accept Christ Jesus as your Lord and Savior. If you have never done this, repeat these simple words with me and it will be a done deal. Repeat with me the following: Lord Christ Jesus as of this very moment, I accept you as Lord and savior of my life. I now give my life to you to be fashioned for your purpose and glory. All these things I have said I truly believe in my heart and have confessed with my mouth. I know now that I have received everlasting life based on the work that Christ will do in my life. Lord Christ, thank you for bringing me to this point of my life where I surrender all to you. It is in the Holy Spirit through Christ Jesus I say Amen.

Humbly Yours in Christ,
Apostle Jamie Pleasant

About the Author

Apostle Jamie T. Pleasant; Ph.D. was born October 9, 1962 in Sumter, South Carolina as an only child to Anthony and Bertha Pleasant. As a modern day polymath, excelling in Physics, Etymology, Business, Personal Finance and Investing, Bible Teaching, Apostleship and Sports, he continues to share his wealth of knowledge to the next generation. His parents were entrepreneurs during the early 1940's and he inherited their spirit of economic development and business ownership at an early age.

At the young age of eight years old, Apostle Pleasant began working in a corner grocery store and also sold Grit newspapers to earn his own money. At 12 years old, after his mother died, he started his first two businesses, owning a landscaping business and refreshment stand. His first year of business brought him more than $5,000 in revenues. At his father's passing, his passion and pursuit to earn a college degree would not be hampered by life's circumstances. He began working odd jobs in the janitorial and restaurant industry at night while attending college in the day to make ends meet.

After obtaining a bachelor's degree in Physics from Benedict College in Columbia, South Carolina, Apostle Pleasant then transferred to Clemson University where he walked on the football team to later earn an athletic scholarship while studying business. He further advanced his education by achieving a M.B.A. in Marketing from Clark Atlanta University. Finally, on August 13, 1999, Apostle Pleasant achieved a Georgia Tech milestone by becoming the first African American to graduate with a Ph.D. in Business Management in the school's 111- year history.

On July 31, 1995, through a successful radio ministry, New Zion Christian Church was birthed. God gave him the vision to establish a Biblically based economic development initiative for the church. As a result, Apostle Pleasant is constantly sought after and he remains at the pulse of the economic business sector.

He created programs in the church such as the Wealth Builders Investment Club (WBIC), which educates and allows members to actively invest in the stock market, along with the much celebrated Institute of Entrepreneurship (IOE), where community members earn a certificate in Entrepreneurship after three months of comprehensive training on aspects of starting and owning a successful competitive business. The main goal and purpose of IOE is that each year one of the trained businesses will be awarded up to $10,000 start up money to ensure financial success. The newly added SAT & PSAT prep courses for children ages 9-19 fuels the potential success of all who walk through the doors of New Zion Christian Church.

Apostle Pleasant has met with government officials such as President Clinton and Nelson Mandela. He has performed marriage ceremonies and counseled numerous celebrated personalities such as Usher Raymond (Confessions Recording Artists), Terri Vaughn (Lavita Jenkins on The Steve Harvey Show), Peerless Price (Atlanta Falcons WR) and many others. He is civically engaged as well. After the Columbine High School shooting; he founded the National School Safety Advocacy Association. His latest foundations include the Young Entrepreneurship Program (YEP) and the African American Consumer Economic Rights Inc (AACER).

Apostle Pleasant is the husband of Kimberly Pleasant and the proud father of three children; Christian, Zion and Nicara.

Made in the USA